presents

Weddings & Honeymoons
in the Vineyards
of
Northern California

By Judith Rivers

Our cover

photograph

was taken

by

Ray Baltar

Robert Pierce Studios

at

B.R. Cohn Winery

Kenwood

California

DEDICATION

Our books are dedicated to those in love and reaching toward commitment to one another through the traditional action of declaration and celebration. May you continue daily to reaffirm one another as your choice for life. May you each consider this commitment to one another as a priority in your daily lives.

Marriage is like a roller-coaster,
you have your ups and downs;
and you have to hang on tight for the curves.
BY, JUDITH RIVERS

We are members of the following visitor's bureaus and chambers of commerce in Northern California.

Napa, Santa Rosa, Sonoma, Russian River, Walnut Creek, Concord, and San Ramon chambers, the Sonoma Convention Bureau, Sonoma Visitors Bureau and the Santa Rosa Convention and Visitors Bureau.

SPECIAL THANKS TO OUR ASSOCIATES

WRITER - PUBLISHER - RESEARCH
Judith Rivers

EDITORIAL ASSISTANTS
Sandy Hensley Nancy Azevedo

ADVERTISING SALES
Judith Rivers

ADMINISTRATIVE ASSISTANTS
Nancy Azevedo

CONTRIBUTING PHOTOGRAPHERS

Ray Baltar	Matthew Kenneally	Michael Loeb	Alta Tawzer
Eileen Fahy	Margretha Lane	Joshua Rotsten	Dennis Urbiztondo
Pam Goslin	Lightworks	Sylvia	

ART AND DESIGN DIRECTOR
Todd Towner of T&H Graphics

PRINTER
Publishers Press ~ Salt Lake City, Utah

INTERMARKET LINKS

NORTHERN CALIFORNIA
WEDDING LINKS
http://weddinglinks.com/

GLOBAL SEARCH
WEDDING LINKS
http://www.a-wedding.com

Ray Baltar - Web Master - Designer
Judith Rivers, Administrator & Marketing
E Mail: jrivers@ap.net

INTRODUCTION

This romantic and picturesque book has been created to provide complete information to couples who want to ELOPE, BRING A LARGE WEDDING CELEBRATION, OR HONEYMOON in the Vineyards of Northern California.

This book provides…

A COLLECTION OF INFORMATION ON WEDDING AND RECEPTION LOCATIONS IN VINEYARD SETTINGS. Situated in wineries, vineyards or within view of the vineyards in the counties of Lake, Napa, Sonoma Mendocino, Contra Costa and Alameda in Northern California.

HONEYMOON LOCATION DETAILS OF ROMANTIC VINEYARD SETTINGS. There are places to stay and plan the enjoyable honeymoon activities in the surrounding areas. All styles and budgets are viewed in the editorials on the following pages.

ROMANTIC ELOPEMENT LOCATIONS are earmarked in the sections called Vineyard Locations and the Nearby Vineyard Locations. Included are locations and services which a couple may contact to help them create their romantic elopement and memorable marriage.

FUN DAY TRIPS to the towns and cities in the area. Included are restaurants, outdoor activity, wineries, romantic places to stay, and guidance to the beautiful wine country. These pages may be used to provide your guests with activities, honeymooners with fun things to do, and eloping couples with romantic settings to make their event an incredible memory.

TABLE OF CONTENTS

- Dedications and Acknowledgments
- Introduction
- Table of Contents

TABLE OF CONTENTS

GUIDANCE AND INFORMATION FOR THE AREA

INTERNET INFORMATION

Many locations have internet web pages listed
in the article written about them.

KEYS TO THE VINEYARD LOCATIONS
TABLE OF CONTENTS
HEARTS   signify elopement locations.
DOVES   signify exceptional locations.

A few locations for both weddings and honeymoons in this
book have been given the term "exceptional". This is a
personal evaluation of the beauty, service and possibilities
the location offers couples.

VINEYARD - WEDDING AND RECEPTION LOCATIONS

TABLE OF CONTENTS

TABLE OF CONTENTS

Keyed sites:

♥ Hearts will handle elopements

💍 Rings are exceptional location

Table of Contents

TABLE OF CONTENTS

VINEYARD HONEYMOONS
IN NAPA COUNTY

VINEYARD HONEYMOONS
IN MENDOCINO COUNTY

TABLE OF CONTENTS

At A Glance

PHASE I – EARLY DECISIONS

_____ Season you will be married   _____ Date - of wedding/of reception

_____ Wedding colors   _____ Wedding party number/who

_____ Engagement in newspaper

Develop your budget which includes the following:

_____ Rings - select   _____ Size of wedding - intimate/large

_____ Formal wear   _____ Style- traditional/modern/formal

_____ Honeymoon   _____ Setting of wedding - inside/outside

_____ Florist/decorations/rentals   _____ Type of refreshment/food

_____ Music/transportation   _____ Photographer/videographer

_____ Any other budgeted items

_____ Area & location of wedding, reception

PHASE II – EARLY SELECTION/RESERVATION

To reserve or order you often need to deposit money. For assurance
of your favorite selections, begin as early as possible:

_____ Bridal consultant

_____ Site - select and reserve: For wedding, for reception(s)

_____ Clergy - select, discuss vows, schedule rehearsal and the counseling - when indicated

_____ Attire for wedding party - select garments or select seamstress

_____ Bride and attendants' schedule

_____ Groom and attendants' schedule

_____ Fittings and select accessories

At A Glance

_____ Photographer- engagement, passport wedding day announcement for
newspaper, outline of what photos you want taken at event

_____ Videographer- select

_____ Florist- select

_____ Determine colors, types and list for both wedding and reception

_____ Refreshments/dinner

_____ Plan food

_____ Style of service, caterer, favors, mints, nuts,

_____ Baker- choose cake

_____ Select music for ceremony, reception

_____ Transportation - to and/or from the wedding/reception

_____ Plan honeymoon - visas passports

PHASE II -ADDITIONAL SELECTIONS
BEGIN EARLY AS POSSIBLE

_____ Ceremony & vows outlined

_____ Guest list - number, obtain lists from families

_____ Printer: select invitations and thank-you's
(allow 8-12 weeks for printing and mail 5-6 weeks before the wedding)

_____ Napkins, ribbons

_____ Sign up at bridal registries

_____ Cake top decoration - select

_____ Mints, candy and nuts

_____ Favors made

_____ Honeymoon - reservations made

_____ Rehearsal and dinner - plans

_____ Wedding breakfast- plans

AT A GLANCE

Purchase:

_____ Gifts for attendants   _____ Toasting goblets

_____ Ring pillow   _____ Cake knife (unless caterer has this)

_____ Garter

Below are additional items you may determine are needed. Some may be rented or are part of other arrangements with consultant, caterer or site. Confirm their availability: tables, chairs, large serving pieces, linens and table place-settings; paper products, balloons, canopies, aisle runner and wine/bar glasses (or plastic); decorations including aisle ribbons, gazebos, arches, plants, candelabra and table decorations.

PHASE III *~*EIGHT WEEKS TO PLAN *Confirm all services with correct date, time, address and your completed requests.*

Finalize the responsibility for:

_____ Invitations addressed, mailed five weeks ahead

_____ Favors made and who will disburse favors

_____ In charge of equipment rentals/borrowed

_____ Deliveries set-ups and return

_____ Guest book

_____ Valet and parking

_____ Special decorations

_____ Reception service and clean-up

_____ Bustle the bride (know who & learn ahead)

_____ Extra snap shots of rehearsal and attendants dressing

_____ Aisle decorations

_____ Tux - pick-up and return

_____ Person to cut the cake

_____ Servers/clean-up for reception

AT A GLANCE

SET THESE DATES

_____ Pre-wedding photos

_____ Fittings for dresses

_____ Fittings for men's tuxes

_____ Hairstylist/try wedding veil

_____ Hairstylist/wedding day

_____ Cosmetics/wedding day

_____ Nails

LAST MONTH TO PLAN

_____ Designate someone to be at wedding site early to handle the following: arrival of cake, flowers, decorations, food and beverage (or service), musicians and gifts.

_____ Confirm honeymoon plans.

_____ Tabulate guest replies - give count to food coordinator/caterer/baker. Sometimes you may have to call guests to get replies.

_____ Log gifts as they are received.

_____ Indicate you have sent thank-yous.

AT A GLANCE

Bring to the Wedding & Reception:
Something Old, Something New, Something Borrowed, Something Blue.

Necessary Items:
Wedding license, minister's fee in envelope, toasting goblets, cake-cutting knife, guest book and pen, rings and ring pillow, garter, flower petals, birdseed or rose petals, scissors, tape for wedding gifts' cards (tape cards to boxes), last minute decorations or photographs to be placed, camera loaded-extra film and batteries.

Lists:
Special photos you want from photographer and videographer, timelines for hostess, caterer, best man, maid of honor and musicians. (These can be mailed ahead of time and brought day of wedding).

Personal items:
Tissues, hair spray, barrettes/pins, brushes, extra nylons, iron, scissors, needle and thread, safety pins, veil, nail care items, underwear, shoes, smelling salts, WEDDING CLOTHING, grocery sacks for attendants' clothing and personal belongings for convenient clean-up.

Honeymoon items:
Purse and wallets, passports, ID's and honeymoon tickets, packed luggage with keys, address book, camera and keys for return home, maps, credit cards, reservation verifications, cash, travel checks and checkbook.

ILLUSTRATIVE TIME LINE

The timeline is helpful if you have no wedding hostess or have a limited amount of time scheduled at the facility. It becomes uncomfortable for the guests to wait more than 10-15 minutes for the ceremony to begin.

Work out your own plan. Ask the minister how long his ceremony usually lasts, then take into account what you have added or deleted in regard to music or readings. The officiate usually manages the time during the wedding. Ask one of your friends to keep you moving prior to the wedding and during the reception by adhering the group to the time line. That person wears a watch and gives a quiet touch of the elbow and whisper in the ear to keep people moving throughout the event.

*Give the plan to a bridesmaid, a groomsman and the photographer. It generally takes the bride two hours at the site to get ready. Some people arrive ready to walk down the aisle. * Items will often be covered at home. Always include the transportation time.*

The following is an illustration:

TIME	WEDDING PARTY	TIME	WEDDING PARTY
*12 noon	arrive at site to get ready	1:45	bride and mother
1:00	flowers distributed to all	1:50	special time for bride & mom
1:00	photographer arrives	*2:00	seat the groom's mother
1:15	groom and attendants' photos	2:10	seat the bride's mother
1:15	groom and family photos	2:10	groom & attendants enter
1:25	bride portraits-train	2:13	special music in ceremony
1:35	bride and attendants		

ILLUSTRATIVE TIME LINE

TIME WEDDING PARTY

2:15	bridal attendants enter
2:17	bride enters with father
2:40	ceremony (20 min to 2 hr.)
3:00	photo session for families
	(this can last longer also)

*May need travel time here with reception
beginning an hour later or more.*

4:00	formal photos - greeting of
	guests with formal reception line
4:15	wedding toast
4:15	food with bride and groom
	leading the way
5:10	signing the documents and
	freshen up
5:15	music begins with bride and
	groom leading the way
6:00	cutting of the cake and serving
6:45	distributing favors
7:00	bridal bouquet toss
7:15	garter thrown - resume dancing
8:45	change clothing
8:45	rose petals/bird seed distributed
9:00	couple leave the event - party continues
1-2 hrs	clean-up (recommend ending party
	prior to closing time of site to
	afford time for clean-up)

At A Glance

PHASE IV
WRITE ON THIS CALENDAR THE LAST
WEEK PRIOR TO THE WEDDING

Seventh day before wedding (date) _____

Sixth day before wedding (date) _____

Fifth day before wedding (date) _____

Fourth day before wedding (date) _____

Third day before wedding (date) _____

Day before your wedding (date) _____

HAPPY WEDDING DAY! (date) _____

SELECTING YOUR WEDDING
& RECEPTION SITES

Deciding where you are to be married entails several basic decisions the couple should make together. Etiquette provides that brides have the priority to select the city and the facility for the wedding, but in today's culture this is most often decided between the bride and groom.

There may be desires which both of you will want to include in a list of priorities for the wedding and reception site. Write them down, discuss each one and place a priority number on each. When you phone the sites for appointments to visit, you may ask questions that will ensure you have your priority considerations at your budgeted price. Sites are often reserved as much as a year ahead. If a chosen site is not available on your desired day, a midweek wedding is very "European" and very much in style today. Many sites give considerable discounts for mid-week events.

Churches, historic sites, parks, gardens and private wooded areas, as well as the usual reception halls and restaurants, are part of the possibilities included in this book.

When selecting the site, consider the following questions:
- What is the guest capacity?
- Is there a site host or hostess available on the chosen date?
- How many hours is the site available to you for rehearsal and/or wedding?
- What are the rules and regulations for using the site?
- What determines the cost of the site?
    a. how many attend event
    b. segment of time used
    c. both
- Is the site location convenient for the majority of your guests?
- What is the deposit and when is it due?

Selecting Your Wedding & Reception Sites

- Is there a place for the wedding party to dress?
- Are restroom facilities adequate?
- Is there handicap access?
- Is there electrical power available?
- Is liability insurance provided or needed?

When selecting a site, consider the following questions:

- If wedding and/or reception are outdoors, what are the provisions for inclement weather?
- Is a one-day alcohol license required for the reception?
- Is the kitchen adequate for the type of food you want to prepare and serve?
- What arrangements should be made for clean-up? Is there an additional fee for this?
- Do you need to rent items for wedding and/or reception? (Many caterers will handle this).
- Some of those items are: linens, punch bowls, dishes, utensils, tables and chairs, gazebos, flower baskets, bar glasses. These items need someone in the wedding party to be responsible for their timely return.

Weddings and receptions are great fun in the homes and yards of family and friends. Mobile home parks and many senior residential areas have available recreation rooms. Bed and Breakfast establishments sometimes provide a complete weekend service to you and your guests. For some, this includes the ceremony, food and decorations and the overnight accommodations for several guests.

Couples can be creative with ceremonies, such as a small private wedding and a large reception. Often with families in different parts of the world there are two receptions. A bridal consultant, family member or friend may handle the distant reception.

How Winery-Vineyard Weddings
are Different

There are approximately six-hundred wineries throughout the five Northern California counties explored in this book. Among these, very few are public about the weddings they do. Your chances are increased in making successful plans by using this publication. Included are bed & breakfasts, hotels, inns, ranches, restaurants, wineries and community halls in the vineyards or in view of the vineyards.

There are many locations that wish to remain exclusive with caterers and consultants which bring them the couples. That is why we offer you a referral line of 707-570-0820. My staff or I will aid you in the process if you are not finding the location of your dreams in this book. Our knowledge of the professionals in the area - and their styles-may help you create a perfect event.

Most wineries refuse to do weddings. They prefer to do corporate events or none at all. Because of their romantic popularity, wineries often book a year to two years in advance; consequently, event availability varies between wineries. While some host mid-week or weekend nuptials and elopements, others make themselves available for one day a month because of other activities on site.

The wineries work within a certain realm of rules. Many of them are working wineries with harvest, bottling and ageing of the wine. They have created beautiful wine-tasting rooms, gardens and patios for guests to enjoy their vintages. Truly the romance of the vineyard is part of the beauty surrounding the wine. Yet wineries are governed by regulations and agricultural acts which pre-determine many of the rules set forth in their contract with couples who desire weddings on their grounds. Other vineyard locations do not deal with as many rules and have been included in this text for your consideration.

How Winery-Vineyard Weddings are Different

The Rules for Wineries - not for other vineyard settings.

• Understand wineries are wine makers first.

• Each county may differ in its event regulations. Various areas of each county may differ in their ability to offer weddings and receptions. This is why the search is very frustrating.

• Winery weddings may begin after the wine-tasting room is closed, (4-5 pm) unless there is a separate area for events.

• They must serve their own wines to encompass their event license legally. New laws do allow some additional beverages. They must adhere to these laws. No hard liquor is allowed.

• Not all wineries have staff to help you coordinate your event. They often recommend a preferred consultant or caterer.

• Fees vary, as do the services included in the fees.

• Some require additional liability insurance which is your responsibility to achieve in order to use the site.

• To our knowledge we have placed event sites with the proper event license in this publication.

Common Rules for Vineyards and Other Locations

• County and city rules for sound abatement after 9:00 p.m. or 10:00 p.m. are not uncommon. Music may need to be indoors only or turned off by a specific time.

• Parking on roads (especially narrow ones) may lead to the need for hiring a shuttle to bring your guests from a pre-designated parking area.

How Winery-Vineyard Weddings are Different

The Elements

- California's rainy season is between November and April as a general rule. We do see short storms in May and an occasional August and early autumn storm. It is recommended you check the Farmer's Almanac for weather projections in and around the dates you are considering. (Or another similar publication and from an internet weather site.)
- Option is.... You can also look for a location with an indoor/outdoor facility or tent the event.
- We have seasons. Winters are from mid November to February. Spring is mid-February through May. We can have extremes of hot weather (100's) or cool (50-60's) from May through October. We rarely have a humid climate. Our evenings do cool down along the coast but the inland areas are warm. The grapevines have no foliage in the winter from December through most of March. Many people love the mustard season in February. There are acres of barren vines with bright yellow mustard growing everywhere, plus pink plum trees and yellow acacia blooming. The vineyards bud forth in April. Our hills are emerald green in winter, then dry to a golden grass by June and do not change until our winter rains begin.

"See the color photo collage pages in this book"

Creature Comforts

- Outdoor heaters are very popular for evening events, as well as umbrella tables during the day for shade.
- The grape crush season between August and October often give off a pungent aroma which some people love and some hate.
- The roads leading to the sites are often narrow and the locations tucked into the hills. This is part of the beauty and romantic ambiance you seek

to achieve. Maps do help your guests find their way to the location. Include them in your invitations. Most locations have pre-designed maps.

• Portable toilet units are not uncommon for events deep in the vineyards and away from buildings.

Finding and Reserving Your Vineyard Location

While most couples under normal circumstances set the wedding date and then find the location(s). The popularity of the vineyards and wineries causes this custom to work in reverse.......

You may decide to pick a season - work well in advance of the year you choose to be married and then find an available location.

There are two apparent avenues of reserving a vineyard location.

• Call several to see if they are available on the date you desire. Then take the time to view the locations and agree upon a contracted date with the location event coordinator.

• Have a consultant or caterer bring you into a location. Decide on a site according to your description/dreams - then find a free date for your wedding.

Many locations do have a preferred list of professionals they work with, so it is wise to make your location and available date a priority decision. All other professionals involved in your event hinge on the location and date of your wedding. If you change this....some of them may not be available for your plans.......or you may be requested to hire a different set of professionals.

How Winery-Vineyard Weddings are Different

Often sites will be flexibile and waive their professional list if you can assure them of the professional standards of the person you want to bring in. They may require that person to interview with them ahead of time and review the site.

The winery settings often include an on-site consultant
This is a key person who acts as liaison between the site and event. With the situation where you want a particular location, you rarely have a choice of a consultant to bring to that location. The coordinator is hired by the location. They are often organized and trained to their position and create events for weddings and the corporate world specific to that location. If you need a personal wedding consultant to help you create your event, then the two work together to bring your event into focus at that location. Locations often have a list of coordinators they love working with.

The on-site coordinator has an in-road to many pre-interviewed wedding professionals they choose to work with. They will make one specific, or a variety of recommendations according to your style and taste. They are staff members and seek to bridge the gap between the brides' requests and the vineyard location rules. Very few places have a "package" where you automatically have to hire someone. Most give you a recommendations list. Please ask the on-site coordinator the parameters of their duties.

- What arrangements do you make for me other than book the location? Do you require me to hire a bridal consultant in order to use the location?
- Are you there on the day of the wedding to aid in the process of the event or is someone else needed for this? Do I call you directly as questions come up?
- Do I hire and individually contract each service or is this a package that I choose from and you finish the details of the event?

Planning A Wedding
From A Distance

New information arrives daily on the internet and in new publications. It is not as easy to plan a distant wedding as it appears, and not as difficult as it was years ago. In spite of the flow of information given today, we can not discount the importance of personal service, a matter of chemistry between you and the people you hire. These are the professionals who will surround you on your wedding day. Taking time to reassure yourself regarding these people will allow you to be calmer the day of your event.

The requirement of trust and being able to let go of a major project into many different professional vendor's hands from afar is difficult for some couples. There are several ways to approach this:

Couples make two to three trips to the area ahead of the planned date to interview and hire the specific people for the important day. While you may be adept at rounding up the "qualified" vendors, it is best to draw upon a book of quality information and/or an informed source such as a consultant.

Other couples like to pick up the phone and say, "I want this, this and this, and I'm leaving the details to you. I will be there at a specific time and I know it will be done." Amazing! They arrive as a guest at their own event and accept what is....this works great if you are eloping but rarely works if planning a wedding for 200 guests.

Though expensive, couples may hire a consultant from where they live to come into the vineyards and create the wedding, but they do not know who to hire without access to the correct area resources.

Some couples rely upon a relative or friend in the area to make the

PLANNING A WEDDING
FROM A DISTANCE

arrangements. This is great if you can depend on them and they follow through as you would and it is not a burden in their schedule. This is time consuming and not fun for some people, so understand you are asking a great deal from them. Purchasing a copy of the same workbook and then relying on phone communication works for this plan.

Hiring a consultant who is knowledgeable of the area you choose to be married in can be a great asset. They will have interviewed the vendors, know the locations, tasted the cakes and be able to create an event from your desires, budget, and individual style. That is what you are paying for....their experience and recommendations, creativity, listening ability and often they save you a great deal of money.

It is very difficult to plan strictly from long distance, arrive the day before and have everything completed to your heart's desire unless you and your consultant are in communication with one another. This usually involves:

- A flurry of conversations, e-mails, faxes to find the right consultant or group of people to help at the other end.
- Several communications to set dates, places, vendors and contracts. Read, review, and pay close attention to tips, taxes, hidden costs, times in and out of the location, overtime for vendors, what each service gives and for what amount of time.
- Keep a log of conversations from your end with dates and notes regarding requests. If you make any changes, additions of guests, or foods....this requires a new price quote.
- There will be a quiet lull of time and then confirmations with the consultant need to be reviewed four weeks prior: Use of "At A Glance" in this book will help considerably.

Planning A Wedding
From A Distance

- Your arrival times, phone numbers where you each may be reached once in the area, etc. should be sent to all concerned in your event. Your attendants and immediate relatives who are involved in the event need an itinerary of how to reach the wedding party, where and if there are pre-wedding gatherings, the rehearsal time and dinner location.

Their lists of vendor's do reflect people who have worked with them and are known for their professionalism.

Hiring A Free Lance
Wedding Consultant

Should you decide to hire a free-lance wedding consultant over the phone who is familiar with the area, there are a few thoughts you may add to this decision making process.

Consider Hiring A Consultant:
• When the wedding is small or large.
• When you are too busy or do not wish to handle details.
• When the planning time is short.
• When you do not have a friend or family member to help you.
• When you are new to the area or planning the wedding a distance from your home.
• When a consultant can keep the flow of the wedding and reception moving and relieve you and your families of overseeing the event, thus allowing more fun.

A consultant's most important asset is to get the job done effectively and cordially. Interview a few consultants early in the planning process. Ask for references and call them. Many consultants are listed by the Association of Bridal Consultants and/or June Wedding Inc.

Note: When you ask a consultant to freely give you recommendations over the phone.....it is similar to asking a CPA for advice free of charge. They have sifted through and found qualified people, locations and need to charge for their time and recommendations.

• They should return your calls within twenty-four to forty-eight hours. (Sundays and Mondays are generally their days off).
• Determine their availability on the specific dates you have in mind.

Hiring a Free Lance Wedding Consultant

- Many give an hour of free consulting or with a minimum charge. This allows you to share:
- What you have in mind for a location, what you envision, think is important, budget, your dreams.
- They should be able to hear your dreams, desires and budget and know if they have the correct resources for you. One cannot expect them to give out pertinent location/resource information without a contract and a deposit made. If you have a specific location in mind...be up front and say, "Can you get me in to that particular location?" The site (location) is often very clear about who they will allow to work on the premises.
- Your first step is to ask for their packet of references and how they do their business, charges, etc. Get the feel of whether you click (she/he understands what you want). Listen for the type of professional experience, years at the profession, how many weddings they do each year. Call references.
- How are the consultant's fees structured? Emphasize the question of what is received for the money spent. Most consultant fees vary in the U.S., some are by the hour, by the event, by what you require them to do. They can vary for the day of the event, some will do every detail, and others have you hunt and contract every little thing from their preferred lists. Most offer a variety of these structures. Remember it is difficult to individually contract each vendor from a long distance, unless you plan to come into the area occasionally.

Other wedding coordinators make themselves available only on the day of the wedding. They see to details the day of and throughout the flow of events. This leaves all else to you.

Coordinators often specialize in elopements, putting together each of the details you desire, as elaborate or simple as you choose. Some will see to your honeymoon suite, marriage license and make ready the site and clergy at this end

HIRING ANY OF THE PROFESSIONALS YOU MAY REQUIRE

- Make a list of questions before you call. If you do not reach the person but must leave a message on a machine, clearly state your name, area code and phone number, plus the best time to call you back.

- Begin with a reputable book, or bridal association in the area. Remember, anyone can advertise in newspapers, magazines or join a chamber or visitors bureau. The telephone book and these forms of marketing do not check out how long a business has been around or their qualifications/references.

- Hiring from the Internet may also have its flaws unless the web producers have the attitude they will place on-line only pre-qualified businesses. Search Engines do not pre-qualify web pages but often the person's web page will example their work and experience and give references.

- No matter how much of a hurry you are in, ask for references and take the time to call them. A few long-distance calls may save you headaches and money.

- Get a contract! If something goes wrong....you have no recourse without a signed contract. Please do not leave messages of importance… changes....problems....or needs on an answering machine without stating, "Call me back to confirm that you received my message".

- It is prudent to leave the best times to reach you when discussing business.

Eloping to the Romantic Vineyards

Elope means to plan a secret trip to get married.

This could be planned out over several months and kept secret, or you may decide all of a sudden to take off and get married.

The elopement can be a quick return trip home to announce to family and friends, or it can include time for a honeymoon with telegrams or phone calls to announce.

Many couples do pre-announce their plan to elope and head for a beautiful romantic setting in some part of the world to exchange their vows and honeymoon at the same time.

This publication will certainly help you with everything concerned. The locations to elope to are keyed with hearts in the front index. It signifies those locations which are known to help you coordinate a ceremony nearby or at their location. You will also see "Elopement" listed in the top of the box on the location text. We have advertised clergy in this book or call our referral line. 707-570-0820, Monday Saturday, Pacific Time 10: am to 9: pm.

Northern California with its vineyards and Pacific coast have become very popular venues for eloping. The ability to bring your wedding license from another state, or arrive on Thursday and get your license Friday morning, makes eloping here easier. The county clerk's phone numbers for each county have been included in the front of this publication. Please read the article on marriage licenses.

Eloping to the Romantic Vineyards

Saturdays are difficult to find locations for elopements compared to Friday evenings, Sunday afternoons or mid-week. The reason is the vineyard locations have been booked well in advance. We have several private locations we can refer you to on the Recommendation Line.

Be certain to bring this book with you. It will allow you to enjoy the many wonderful things available in the area by the quick referencing of great things to do and see while in the vineyards.

A retreat wedding is with a small group of friends and/or family.

A retreat wedding is planned so that others may break away from their schedules and join you at a special location reserved in advance. It can include bringing several close friends or a few family members to the chosen spot to witness and celebrate and spend vacation time together.

PLANNING YOUR HONEYMOON IN THE VINEYARDS

You will find the variety, romance and beauty most couples look for when planning a honeymoon in our Northern California's vineyard areas. Some of the finest chefs in the world reside in these lovely locations. The hotels, bed and breakfast venues and lovely inns hold romance and privacy as the highest priority for their guests. The prices and accommodations vary so you will find something perfect for your budget.

As you use this book and explore the possibilities of great honeymoon locations, be certain to read the chapters on Day Trips. Make reservations ahead of time from the "Day Trip or Honeymoons articles.. It is important to reserve ahead. Weekends are often reserved months in advance in our areas, but honeymooners will find mid-week is easier to obtain.

There are many camping spots in this area. Couples love this possibility. Please call our referral number for ideas should you choose this venue, or get on the internet for the California State Parks system. There are many types of camping offered here. Private, city, county and state. One or two actually look onto vineyards.

Included in this book are day trips into San Francisco and along the Pacific coast to extend your adventures. Even if you hate wine, you will find great things to do in each of the "Day Trip" areas outlined. The excellent opportunity to rest or see as much as you choose is at hand. Exciting San Francisco is at your beck and call, the drama of the rocky Pacific coast and sound of the waves, plus the greatest outdoor activities are easily available from these pages. You can make arrangements ahead of time from this text. The book is intended to be kept with you at all times throughout your trip and planning.

MARRIAGE LICENSES

If coming from a foreign country, you must take out your marriage license in the local county in which you plan to be married. Always check with the county clerk or official in your area for restrictions on this.

It is recommended you call the county clerk's office of the location you are planning to go to. If coming from a foreign country please clear local rules about being married on foreign soil. You will be required here to have passports, birth certificates and possibly other documentation - depending on the county in the USA.

If coming from California, you may bring a license from another county. From a state in the U.S. call your county clerks offic and ask for stipulations and then call the vinyards county clerks' office where you plan to be married for details.

If you need a marriage license, you will need to arrive before Friday and be in the County Clerk's office early Friday. Check for holidays on those Thursday-Fridays...sometimes government offices are closed.

You must always bring:
• Bring proof of who you are. Passport, drivers license, etc.
• If married previously, bring your divorce papers and the above.
• Make certain your marriage license is signed by the officiate and that they send this to the appropriate authority. You will need a copy of your new marriage license also.

WEDDING PLANNING WORK PAGES FOR DISTANCE PLANNING

Chosen Location _____

Physical Address _____
On-Site contact _____
Phone _____
Fax _____

Consultant Name _____
Address _____
City _____ zip _____
Phone _____
E-Mail _____
Fax _____

Location for our stay prior to wedding _____
Address _____
Phone _____
E mail address _____
Fax _____

Reservation dates _____

Location for rehearsal dinner _____
Address _____
Phone _____
E mail address _____
Fax _____

WEDDING PLANNING WORK PAGES
FOR DISTANCE PLANNING

Reservation date _____

Time _____

Location for our first honeymoon night _____

Address _____

Phone _____

E mail address _____

Fax _____

Reservation date _____

Location for our Honeymoon _____

Address _____

Phone _____

E mail address _____

Fax _____

Reservation date _____

Vendor Contacts
Quick view of Those Participating

	NAME	ADDRESS	PHONE NUMBER
Bridal Apparel			
Bridal Accessories			
Caterer			
Clergy			
Consultant			
Decorations			
Favors			
Florist			
Formal Wear			
Gift Registries			
Invitations			
Marriage License info			
Music/musicians			
Out of town lodgings			
Personal Grooming:			
Hair			
Nails			
Etc.			
Etc.			
Photography			
Transportation			
Videography			
Other			
Other			

Alameda

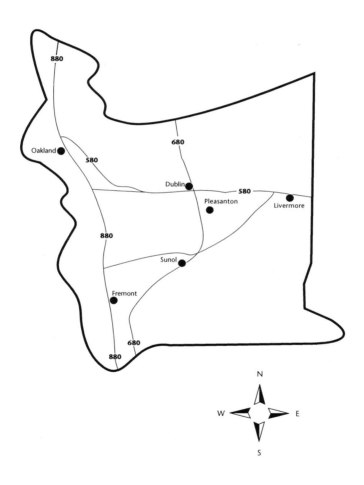

LAKE

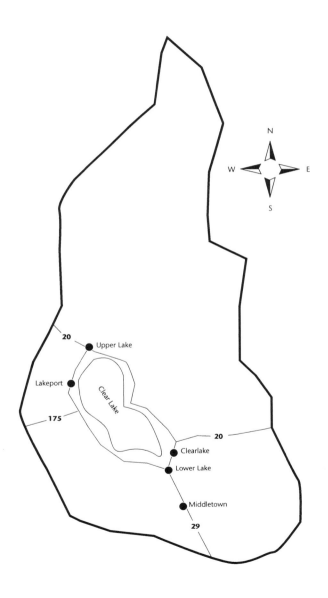

MENDOCINO

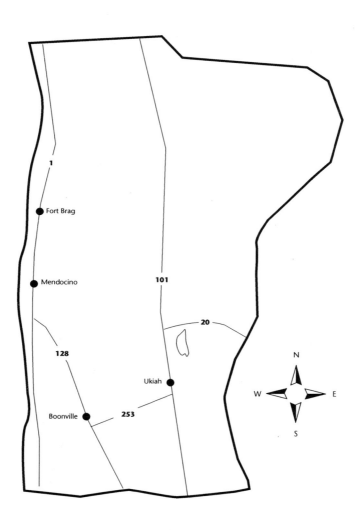

NAPA

Sonoma

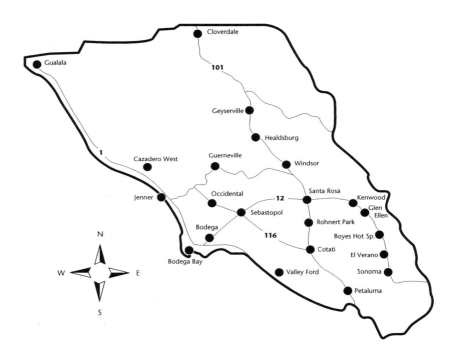

GUIDANCE AND INFORMATION FOR THE AREA

Transportation Services for the Wine Country Areas

San Francisco Airport...415-266-9420

S.F. Immigration/Customs................................415-876-2816

S.F. Traveler's Aid...415-877-0118

Oakland Airport...510-577-4000

Customs...415-744-7741

Immigration...415-705-4411

Traveler's Aid...510-444-6834

S.F.O. Ground Transportation Hot Line...............415-876-2377

Oakland Ground Transportation........................510-658-5400

Napa County Airport..(Napa)...........................707-224-0887

Sonoma County Airport...................................707-524-7240

Mendocino Airport..(Ukiah).............................707-467-2817

Greyhound Bus...800-231-2222

Amtrak...(train)...800-872-7245

Budget Rent-A-Car 800-527-0700

Pure Luxury Limousine...................................800-626-5466

Evans Charter Tours......................................707-255-1557

Western Charter Tours...................................707-763-6815

Weather in the Bay Area.................................415-936-1212

U.S. Passport Office (SF)................................415-744-4010

Emergencies ~ Laws ~ Customs Concerns

Emergency for fire, theft, injury..911

Car Phone dial area code plus..911

Sonoma~Napa~Mendocino...707-911

San Francisco~Marin...415-911

Contra Costa~Oakland~Alameda..510-911

Drinking Age in California is twenty-one.
Expect to be carded (asked for your drivers license), even if at a wine tasting room, wedding or reception if you appear young. Children are not served alcohol and it is frowned upon if you give them sips from your glass.

Responsible Driving Tips
Roads are narrow and winding in some areas of the wine country. Following these safety tips will help:

> Hire a car and driver, take a special tour bus or designate one person as the driver for each car so companions may enjoy the wine tasting and be safe.

> Be careful where you park your car. Blue wheelchair painted on the pavement, yellow or red curbs are a NO.

B&B and Hotel Reservations should be made in advance. Most locations are booked in advance during the summer and fall. Mid-week is often not a problem except holidays.

Tipping in Northern California is customary at 15 to 20% of the amount of your bill. If you have a two for one coupon for item, tip on the full amount without the discount. Some restaurants add on a 15% automatically if you have a group of five or more....please check the bill.

Emergencies - Laws - Customs Concerns

Taxes vary in the wine country from 6% to 12%. Sales tax is 7.25% and hotels tax at a variety of rates according to their community.

Banks are generally open from 10:a.m. until 3 or 5:p.m. Monday through Friday and some on Saturday Mornings till 1:p.m.

Wedding Licenses may be obtained Monday through Friday. Except Holidays. Please read the article in this book pertaining to items you may need and requirements.

You may bring an out of state wedding license to California to be married, but not out of the country. Please call for details at the following or check with American Embassy if coming from another country.

Alameda County License Clerk..510-272-6789

Contra Costa License Clerk...510-646-2986

Lake County License Clerk..510-263-2311

Mendocino License Clerk..707-463-4370

Napa County License Clerk...707-253-4246

Sonoma County License Clerk..707-527-3700

http://www.a-wedding.com

GET OUT OF THE QUAGMIRE AND INTO
THE FAST LANE WITH OUR INTERNET
WEDDINGLINKS GLOBAL SEARCH

"your speed-way to wedding & event information on the net"

As of this date June 97, there are over 1,500 pages regarding businesses and services around the world in our exciting **Wedding Search Directory (engine)**. Businesses from all over the world are understanding how important it is to have their web pages in this search creation by Ray Baltar of InterMarket Links.

Can you imagine.....deciding you want a honeymoon or wedding/event business in a specific place in the world.

typing in the http://www.a-wedding.com and then typing in the (need) photographer, city, state, country....and the search directory (engine) will find those specific to your requests.

This will bring up a menu of the various pages you may look at and click on.... from the business in that specified area who have placed themselves in this exciting search directory.

Should you have E Mail, Fax, or Phone you can reach that business and set appointments, ask for further details than the digital brochure offers. Check their references given. Even hire them to handle your event ...even tho you are nearby or thousands of miles away. Everything would be waiting for your arrival.

This is happening today as you read this!
Enter in..........see what its all about!

We will soon see thousands of wedding/event and honeymoon based businesses in this directory. But It will be quick and easy for all to search and find the business you want to work with because of the rapid search directory. Enjoy your visits.

**Global Search by Internet WeddingLinks has solved the
bog-down issues that other internet sites have.**

**E Mail ~ Staff@a-wedding.com
Phone ~ 707-545-5088**

http://www.weddinglinks.com/

Enter WeddingLinks - Northern California Honeymoon Drawing.

**Show the world your wedding photo
and date in WeddingLinks.**

Our world is becoming smaller as the internet gives us targeted information faster, more complete, and on a daily basis. Just print it out at your printer. The internet has, and is increasing in methods for faster ways to access and move through information.

Internet **WeddingLinks Northern California** provides you with beautifully designed pages and business who are highly qualified to bring you a happy, well thought out event in the Northern California area.

Vineyards, San Francisco. Bay, Coastline, Redwoods

Emphasis on wedding locations in the areas will bring about a quick search for the perfect place to be married. Information derived from the research created by "The Beautiful Weddings Books" is on-line.

Ray Baltar has created web pages with a photographers eye for your enjoyment as you learn more about each business, service or location.

Accessing the Net:
Public libraries, Schools and colleges, Places
of employment, Friends and family

Be in touch:
E Mail - InterMarket Links Staff@a-wedding.com
Phone - 707-545-5088
Fax - 707-539-3556

NOTES

WEDDINGS

IN

VINEYARD

SETTINGS

ELLISTON VINEYARDS
SUNOL ~ ALAMEDA COUNTY

Beneath the Pleasanton Ridge in the beautiful Sunol Valley sits the scenic estate of Elliston Vineyards. Beauty, privacy, excellent food, wine, service and attention to detail are all part of the quality you will receive at this grand facility. The grounds are planted with lawn and rose gardens and vineyards surround the historic stately mansion.

The spacious Terrace Room provides an elegant wedding reception setting for larger groups of 50 to 250. The room sits adjacent to a beautiful deck and gazebo nestled under the hundred year old oak trees. After the ceremony, the couple's head table can be placed in the gazebo for full view by the guests. Fieldstone terraces hold an abundance of flowers and umbrella tables provide shade on the deck.

A lovely, latticed redwood arbor is available on the lawn for ceremonies. The mansion, vineyards and gardens backdrop your photos. Very charming. The Captains's room a private bedroom in the mansion, is available for the bride and her attendants use.

PHOTO BY ELLISTON

The 17 room, three story mansion is available for dinner in many of the private dining rooms at 7 pm These rooms hold 6 to 30 guests for smaller receptions and are excellent for rehearsal dinners. Tours, hors d'oeuvres and champagne are part of the welcoming. An opportunity to meet Elliston's chef Tony Cerny comes later in the evening. He prepares the beautiful foods for both this dining and larger events on the eight acres.

Elliston produces excellent champagne and other fine varietal wines for your reception.

PHOTO BY ELLISTON

LOCATION ACCOMMODATES

- Weddings and Receptions
- Mansion 6 - 30 guests
- Terrace Room 50 - 250 guests
- On-site coordinator for day of event.
- A Preferred Wedding Services list is available
- Music: sound levels - monitored
- Alcohol: Elliston wines and champagne Beer possible. No hard liquor
- Parking: ample
- Deposits: $500 to secure date.
- Fees: 50% due 90 days prior to event details with on-site coordinator
- Insurance: N/A

Phone: 510-862-2377
Fax: 510-862-0316
Internet http://www.tdl.com/ ~elliston
E mail:
Address: 463 Kilkare Road, Sunol, CA 94586

60 minutes from the Oakland Bridge. A map is provided for your guests.

- See the Day Trips section of this book for fun things to do while in the area.

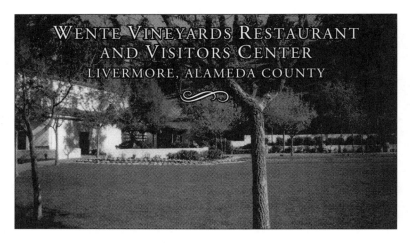

WENTE VINEYARDS RESTAURANT AND VISITORS CENTER
LIVERMORE, ALAMEDA COUNTY

Exceptional settings, gardens and exciting cuisine will sum up your memory of this outstanding location. Wente purchased and restored the former Crest Blanca Winery in 1981. Vineyards were replanted on the canyon floor. Flower gardens and lawns were established to complete the oasis. Historic buildings were carefully restored to the early California elegance of the Spanish mission-style of white stucco and red tiled roofs.

Very large weddings may be accommodated on the grassy lawn. This setting is surrounded by colorful and well-kept flower beds. Majestic palm trees accent the buildings. The area may be tented or tables with umbrellas serve well. Evening lighting is provided for those warm summer evenings. A white lattice arch for ceremonies can be provided, as well as dressing rooms, parking attendants, toasting glasses and wedding cake. A wedding coordinator is available for your rehearsal and event.

Smaller groups may use the tasting room and nearby banquet room. This room opens onto a charming tree shaded patio.

The award winning restaurant has several private rooms which open to terraces for smaller events and rehearsal dinners. The freshest seasonal ingredients are offered and the gardens on the grounds produce the herbs and many fresh items. Wente Vineyards has been winning awards for their still and sparkling wines for decades. Exceptional white wines include Chardonnays, Sauvignon Blanc, and Johannisberg Riesling. Notable red varietal wines include Maerlot, Pinot Noir and Cabernet Sauvignon. Sparkling wines are Brut and Grande Reserve (champagnes) are a must for your toast and celebration. The service provided by the staff at this lovely facility is excellent. They see to the details and you have the fun.

LOCATION ACCOMMODATES

- Weddings and Receptions, Indoor/Outdoor
- Specific areas available year round.
- Visitors Center 200 seated guests
- Restaurant 24 to 200 seated guests
- Lawn and Gardens 300 to 800 guests
- Time: two sessions l0:00am to 3:00pm, 6:00pm to 11:00pm
- A Preferred Services list is available.
- Caterer: in-house
- Tables, chairs, linens and silver are provided.
- Music: amplified permitted - sound monitored
- Alcohol: Wente Wines & Champagne. Selected beers
- Parking: ample
- Deposits: required to reserve date
- Fees: upon request

Phone: 510-447-3023, Catering Department
Fax: 510-447-0970
Internet:
E mail:
5050 Arroyo Road, Livermore, CA 94550

60 minutes from the Oakland Bay Bridge. Your guests may stay at Pleasanton Hilton, Evergreen B&B, San Ramon Marriott, Holiday Inn, or th Pleasanton Sheraton, Rehearsal Dinners may be planned at Elliston Vineyards, Pleasanton Hotel, Uncle Yu's, Bighorn Grill or Wente Bros Restaurant.

Conrad Viano Winery & Vineyards
MARTINEZ ~ CONTRA COSTA COUNTY

This green-belt of vineyards is the last vineyard of fifteen which once grew in this area of Contra Costa County. Family owned and run with the sons of Clement and Sharon Viano, Sharon lends a welcome hand to weddings and receptions and other events to their redwood and pine shaded picnic area.

The gentle hillsides of this area have produced fine grapes and excellent vintages for years. A naturally fermented champagne, "Viano Vineyards", available to guests in addition to other wines. This warm sunny area of California often experiences warm enjoyable outdoor evenings.

No doubt this setting is for a less formal event, but there is room and hospitality for a fun filled occasion. Umbrella tables of redwood with benches may be used or bring in your own style. Oak barrels and a decorated arch for the bride and groom are part of the view with the vineyard as the

backdrop. A bbq, water and power are nearby to aid the caterer. The patio is offered for the dance floor.

This family winery brings the flavor of old Italy to the fields of Martinez.

LOCATION ACCOMMODATES

- Weddings and Receptions
- Outdoor Events only 100 - guests
- Season: April through October
- Time: inquire
- A preferred Wedding Services list is available
- Music: audio levels - monitored
- Alcohol: Conrad Viano wines and champagne
- Parking: ample
- Deposits: upon reservation of date
- Fees:
- Insurance:

Phone: 510-228-6465
Internet
E mail:
Address:150 Morello Avenue, Martinez, CA 94553

1 hour from the Oakland Bridge A map is needed for your guests. Your guests may stay at Muir Lodge, Days Inn, or John Muir Inn. Rehearsal dinners may be planned at Le Beau's or Amato's in Martinez or Le Paradise in Pinole.

- See the Day Trips section of this book for fun things to do while in the area.

GUENOC AND LANGTRY ESTATE
MIDDLETOWN ~ LAKE COUNTY

Romantic weddings and receptions with exceptional memories are being held at the Guenoc and Langtry Estate Chardonnay Vineyards in Lake County near Middletown. The beautiful, historical Victorian ranch home, formerly built and owned by the famous Lillie Langtry, dates back to the 1890's and is the backdrop for wedding ceremonies. The two-story century-old home sits under tall oaks on lawns. As guests enjoy the views and admire this lovely setting, the bride may descend the staircase from the top veranda to the grassy lawn and her waiting groom.

The 300 acre estate vineyard is part of a 23,000 acre ranch located in Guenoc Valley. Several parts of the property may be used for weddings and receptions. Among them is a delightful gazebo in the Victorian garden under the oaks. The bride and her attendants are afforded the use of the lovely Lillie Langtry Room, and Fred Gebhard Room to prepare for the ceremony. These rooms are decorated in late Victorian and Edwardian style. Photo perfect.

The nearby Gebhard Hunting Lodge has a rustic hunter's flair with stone and quartz fireplaces plus rich wood hues and leather furnishings. Both buildings are equipped with modernized kitchens, professional stoves, utensils and wine glasses for events. There are a pool and bbq nearby. Guenoc's Huston Hall is decorated with beautiful chandeliers, wall sconces and portraits from the Lillie Langtry era. This is a large meeting room used for weddings and other events. Views from this spot are of the Guenoc Lake and arbor which is covered in early spring with wisteria and later in the summer with trumpet vine blossoms.

Orville Magoon now owns the vineyards which produce some of the finest wines in the world. They have won numerous world and national awards. The Bordeaux style wines are reds of cabernet sauvignon, petit verdot and merlot, cabernet franc and malbec and Port made from the zinfandel and petite sirah. Many are aged from 18 to 20 months in oak barrels.

LOCATION ACCOMMODATES

- Weddings and Receptions
- Langtry House - outdoor lawn - 100 guests
- Lodge Facilities includes the pool - guests
- Winery/Huston Hall - 80 guests
- Overnight accommodation for wedding party and guests. Can accommodate up to 25 guests.
- Season: year round (no major holidays)
- Time: 10:am and 7:pm
- In-house Catering by Guenoc Winery-Chef
- A Preferred Wedding Services list is available.
- Music: audio - monitored for sound levels
- Alcohol: Guenoc and Langtry wines only.
- Parking: ample
- Deposits: 25% of entire fee to hold location date, 50% of total food and beverage required 30 days prior, $500 security deposit due one week prior
- Fees: upon request
- Insurance:

Phone: 707-987-2385, Hospitality Coordinator
Fax: 707-987-9351
E mail: info@guenoc.com
Address: 21000 Butts Canyon Road, Middletown, CA 95461

2 hours from the Golden Gate Bridge. A map is needed for your guests. Your guests may stay, Konocti Harbor Resort, or South in Calistoga at Christopher Inn, Dr. Wilkersons or Roman Spa and The Pink Mansion. Rehearsal dinners may be held on the Langtry site, Konocti Harbor Restaurant, or All Seasons in Calistoga

- See the Day Trips Section of this book for fun things to do while in the area.

FETZER VINEYARDS AT VALLEY OAKS
HOPLAND ~ MENDOCINO COUNTY

Fetzer Vineyards has opened their beautiful property to weddings, receptions and honeymooners. Located in the heart of Mendocino county near Hopland, this well maintained working winery offers a multitude of possibilities. The extrodianary beauty of this property would enhance any couple's dream of a dream wedding or honeymoon.

The buildings are historic to look like a Kentucky horse farm. Beautifully maintained with soft country greens and white trim. They include an arbored patio, tasting room, and gift store and wine country deli. Daytime you may hold ceremonies and celebrations under the 300 year old Valley Oaks on the Hass House Lawn where umbrella tables may be set up. Overlooking Lake Fume' is an octagon-shaped pavilion with floor to ceiling windows giving an outdoor feeling to a protected event. This is a lovely room with a huge serving bar, wood hues, and perfect for a smaller events and rehearsal dinners.

Fetzer is the location for a starlight wedding. The Arbor area is available with dance floor, stage, outdoor lighting and picnic tables. The warm evenings in this area add to enjoyable summer evening and autumn weddings.

The bed and breakfast looks out over the vineyards and enjoys privacy from the rest of the property. The B&B has 4 guest rooms, 2 suites and a swimming pool. It is made available to the wedding couple and guests for a discounted price. A continental breakfast is provided each morning. Needless to say, it is an perfect retreat wedding location and an excellent romantic honeymoon spot.

The Fetzer Winery produces excellent wines, including Barrel-aged Cabernet, Merlot, Chardonnay, Gewurztraminer, and Bonterra organic wines.

The gardners have created an enormous five acre organic garden to stroll through. Vegetables, herbs and flowers are grown to peak alongside the various fruit trees and berries. Over 1,000 varitys are grown. The Fetzers began a culinary research center with John Ash, the famous chef, teaching classes to now-famous chefs in the lovely Pavilion since 1984.

LOCATION ACCOMMODATES

- Weddings - Receptions
- Retreat Weddings - Honeymoons
- Haas House Lawn - Outdoor Only, 300 guests
- Pavilion - Indoor with adjacent lawn - 80 guests
- Arbor - Outdoor - 160 guests
- Season: year round
- Time: a variety of times available
- Requires: event Consultant
- A Preferred Wedding Services list is available.
- Music: sound levels - monitored
- Acohol: Fetzer Wines offered at a disount
- Parking: ample
- Deposits: upon reservation of date
- Fees: $1800 to $2500 includes 6 hours security guard
  plus Fetzer B&B - discounted accomodations
- Insurance:

Phone: 707-744-7436, Renee Ackerman • 707-744-1250, Office
Internet: www.fetzer.com
E mail: Ranec_ackevman@b-f.com
Address: 13601 East Side Road, Hopland, CA 95449

Two hours from the Golden Gate Bridge. A map is needed for your guests. Your guests may stay at the Thatcher Inn, Sanford House B&B, Vichy Springs Resort. Rehearsal dinners Vichy Springs, Thatcher Inn, Fetzer

- See the Day Trips section of this book for fun things to do while in this area.

Scharffenberger Cellars
Booeville ~ Mendocino County

The majesty of redwoods surrounds your beautiful event at the Scharffenberger Vineyards and redwood grove. A drive out through the vineyards in horse and carriage to the grassy knoll of eight-hundred year old giants is part of the fun. This is where your guests will begin to experience the beauty of what you have planned to share with them on your wedding day. Unforgettable memories are in this unforgettable setting.

There is a bbq, stage and a carriage or antique car to transport guests to the rewood grove. Prior to and during the event, the on-site consultant will guide you throughout the process and carry out your details for the celebration.

An elegant indoor reception area is provided for smaller weddings or rehearsal dinners. The main room is dominated by a massive fireplace. The side doors open onto a deck overlooking acres of vineyards and the nearby hillsides. This artfully decorated area provides a dining room and two fully equipped kitchens for a caterer's use. It is an exquisite portion of their 35,000 square foot building designed by Ulman and Associates in Sausalito, CA.

The Scharffenberger Champagne is considered among the best in California and has won several awards each year. They produce Brut NV, Blanc de Blancs, Brut Rose' and Cremant. The Cremant was created for serving at the White House in 1988.

LOCATION ACCOMMODATES

- Weddings - Receptions -
- Rehearsal Dinners
- Redwood grove - 150 guests
- Winery Reception Area - 50 guests
- Season: April through October
- A Preferred Wedding Services list is available.
- Music: sound levels - monitored
- Alcohol: Scharffenberger Cellars Champagne and other fine Scharffenberger wines
- Parking: ample
- Deposits: 50% to reserve date
- Fees: Redwood Grove $1,000 Winery Reception area $500.
- Insurance: not required

Phone: 800-824-7754, Wedding Coordinator: Deborah Kanani
Internet: http://www.schafffenberger.com

Address: 8501 Highway 128, Philo, CA 94566

Two hours from the Golden Gate Bridge. A map is needed for your guests.

Your guests may stay at the Boonville Hotel, Philo Pottery Inn, and Albion River Inn. Rehearsal dinners at the Winery, Little River or Albion River Restaurants.

- See the Day Trips section of this book for fun things to do while in this area.

AUBERGE DU SOLEIL
"The Inn of the Sun"
RUTHERFORD, NAPA COUNTY

PHOTO BY AUBERGE

Nestled calmly in a terraced olive grove and looking out over miles of vineyards in the Rutherford area of Napa Valley is the extraordinary Auberge du Soleil. Escape, total privacy and the intimacy of having a beautiful spot to share is an important part of the allure of Auberge du Soleil.

The 52 rooms and suites, each with a terrace, reflect the French ambiance and Mediterranean influence. Gardens, pathways and fine art sculptures, wildlife, meandering pathways and serenity are part of the romance. Tennis courts, swimming pool, an exceptional spa service and exercise room and an award winning restaurant bring guests out into the social atmosphere.

Auberge Du Soleil handles elopements, retreat weddings, and receptions on a larger scale with their fine staff and renowned chef, Andrew Sutton. He brings his exceptional recipes and flavorful presentation to cocktail receptions, magnificent celebration feasts and joyful desserts.

A recently created ceremony deck will accommodate 30 seated guests and 130 guests standing. Beautiful views of the Napa Valley are the backdrop of your wedding photographs. There are three other reception rooms, each with its individual charm. Every detail will be drawn together with your decisions and their talented catering department. Important selections for music, place cards, flowers and the perfect wedding cake are all part of the coordinating efforts offered to couples planning a wedding and/or reception.

All guests and especially honeymooners are thrilled to find twenty-four hour room service, privacy, huge tubs some with Jacuzzi, terry cloth robes, a wine and cheese stocked refrigerator in each suite, flowers, fireplaces, beautiful linens and comforters. A exercise room, plus a full service beauty salon, is on site. This is, in my opinion, one of the top ten honeymoon locations in the world. Exceptional

LOCATION ACCOMMODATES

- Weddings - Receptions - Honeymoons
- Elopements - Retreat - Out of town guests.
- Season: Year round, indoor/outdoor
- From 12 to 225 guests
- Cedar Room 40 seated guests
- Vista I 100 seated guests
- Vista II 65 seated guests
- Terrace and Ceremony Deck 225 standing guests
- Time Available: flexible
- Music: sound levels - monitored
- Alcohol: full bar service
- Parking: attendant for larger events
- Deposits: required upon reservation
- Fees: packet upon request

Phone: 707-963-1211
Phone: 707-963-1213 - Restaurant
E mail: AubergDuSolei@AOL.com
180 Rutherford Hill Road, Rutherford, CA 94573

60 minutes from Golden Gate Bridge. A map is needed for your guests. Your guests may stay at Yountville Inn & Spa, Napa Valley Lodge, Harvest Inn, Mansion Fleurie, Rehearsal dinners may be held at Auberge Du Soleil, Pinot Blanc, Napa Valley Grill, Greystone Cellars.

- See the Day Trips section of this book for fun things to do while in the area.

BONAVENTURA BALLOON COMPANY
NAPA COUNTY

The versatility of planning a wedding around a beautiful hot-air balloon was amazing as Joyce Bowen explained how many different events over the years have been created. Joyce is a certified minister, as well as a very experienced and well-trained balloon pilot. Her skills as an event coordinator stand her well as she takes calls from all over the world from those who want a very unique wedding.

With her services, she will find you lodging, take photos or find another photographer. She is adept at making arrangements for a reception site, caterer and pull together whatever you may believe is important, including flowers and music.

For two or two-hundred, the completeness of her services will certainly bring you securely through a beautiful wedding day.

Some couples love to hold the ceremony on the ground as the balloon billows like a bejeweled kaleidoscope in the background or overhead

Joyce stated they come to be married in a variety of outfits. Jeans, tuxedos, silk, satin and pretty dresses, top hats and sun glasses. Many enjoy wearing the historical garb from the era when balloons were the rage, the 1800's. Couples often plan a theme wedding around the balloon and ask guests to wear a costume.

Bonaventura has baskets which hold three to eight persons so you may bring a best man and maid of honor or parents. The bird's eye view of the vineyards is noted with first-hand knowledge of the valley, its vineyards and owners. Seasons of the year will change the colors below. It is a beautiful and exciting experience.

The basket is gaily decorated with ribbons and flowers. Often the ceremony is performed on the ground with friends and family in attendance. After the "I Do's", Joyce soars the couple over the valley of vineyards and brings them back to a very active reception. For elopements, dinner reservations are made and limos or antique cars are ordered for a wine tour.

LOCATION ACCOMMODATES

- Weddings and Receptions
- Elopements and Honeymoon fun
- Balloons 3 to 8 guests each
- Ground Events 200 or more - guests
- Season: dependent on weather
- Time: varies
- Bridal consultant
- A Preferred Wedding Services list is available
- Music: monitored - depending on event site
- Alcohol: not in-flight
- Parking: depending on event site
- Deposits: 50% deposit
- Fees: upon request
- Insurance: dependent on site

Phone: Joyce Bowen, 800-Fly NAPA or 707-944-2822
Fax: 707-944-2220
Address: 133 Wall Rd., Napa, CA 94558

1 hour from the Golden Gate Bridge. A map is needed for your guests. Your guests may stay at Meadowood, Napa Marriotts, Harvest Inn. Rehearsal dinners at Auberge du Soleil, Rutherford Grill or Domaine Chandon.

- See the Day Trips section of this book for fun things to do while in the area.

CHARDONNAY GOLF CLUB
NAPA ~ NAPA COUNTY

One of the finest Northern California golf courses is home to a splendid location for weddings and receptions. The Chardonnay Golf Club was developed in the early 1980's. A beautiful belt of green golf links sits amongst the acres of Chardonnay vineyards. This is the first thing your guest will see as they drive through the elegant gates. Flower beds, ponds and resplendent views embellish this location.

There are spacious rooms in this California Ranch-style building. It has a vaulted ceiling giving an indoor - outdoor feeling. Selected woods bring a rich luster to the inside walls.

The Chardonnay Room is an octagonal shaped room. Very unique and lined with windows looking out upon the golf course and distant vineyards. This room accommodates 70 guests.

The Trophy Room features beautiful chandeliers mounted in the vaulted ceiling. This is a very nice setting for 150 guests. The Members Bar & Grill has a magnificent mahogany bar and hand chiseled stone fireplace which brings a warmth and friendliness to guest in this intimate setting for 50. Combining the two rooms will enable a couple to enjoy hosting 200 guests.

The excellent staff will work with you to arrange the wedding of your dreams. Details of your event will be covered with the catering staff in order to make your day one of happy memories. Meals are created from a variety of cultural dishes by Chef Francisco Aguilar. They encompass special presentations of salmon, beef, chicken, duck and veal. The foods are presented colorfully with the freshest of local ingredients. Buffet or seated the staff promises a great experience for family and friends.

PHOTO BY LIGHTWORKS

LOCATION ACCOMMODATES

- Weddings and Receptions
- Indoors: Chardonnay Room - 70 guests, Trophy Room - 150 guests, Members' Bar & Grill - 50 guests, Combined guests - 200
- Season: year round
- Time: inquire
- In-House Catering
- A Preferred Wedding Services list is available.
- Music: monitored - for audio levels
- Alcohol: Full bar, wine list, champagnes
- Parking: ample
- Deposits: required to hold date
- Fees: upon request of packet
- Insurance:

Phone: Sales & Catering, Dale Lanctot, 707-252-5984
Phone: office number, 707-257-1900
Fax: 707-257-0613
Internet: www.chardonnaygolfclub.com
E mail:cgcgolf@chardonnaygolfclub
Address: 2555 Jamieson Canyon Rd., Napa, CA

45 minutes from the Golden Gate Bridge A map is needed for your guests. Your guests may stay at Silverado Country Club, Best Western Inn in Napa or Napa Marriotts. Rehearsal dinners may be held at LaBoucane French Grill, Downtown Joes, Villa Romano or on the Napa River or The Napa River Boat.

- See the Day Trips section of this book for fun things to do while in the area.

CHARLES KRUG WINERY
ST. HELENA ~ NAPA COUNTY

Some of the largest weddings and receptions have been held at the spacious Charles Krug Winery grounds in St. Helena. The 1881 Carriage House is surrounded by lawns and shaded by the hundred year old oak trees known to this area. Two thousand guests can be accommodated on the two acres of lawns. There is room for a tented area on the lawn if needed. Outdoor lighting is available.

The Carriage House is excellent for serving beautiful foods and dancing, or holding smaller more intimate events inside when weather is unpredictable. The romance of the oak casks in this room surrounds your guests with a working winery ambiance. This can be beautifully decorated with tables, candles and garlands of flowers.

The terrain is fairly smooth and flat for those with walking concerns. A side access road allows for a horse-drawn carriage or car. A large stage with lighting and sound is on the grounds. There are several ceremony areas, but the favorite is on the lawn in front of the magnificent wooden doors of the Carriage House.

Charles Krug founded the winery in 1861. This is considered the oldest winery in the Napa Valley. The buildings are over a hundred years old. Since 1943 the winery has been run by members of the Mondavi family since 1943. They produce 15 different varietals including chardonnays and cabernets.

The winery sits across from the castle-like building owned by the Culinary Institute of America at Greystone. The vineyards are at the edge of this lovely setting. All views give forth a European elegance not afforded to other locations.

The winery does very few weddings and must be booked well in advance.

LOCATION ACCOMMODATES

- Weddings and Receptions
- Indoor Carriage House - 200 guests, 9:am to midnight
- Outdoor Lawn - over 1,000 guests, 9 am to 10 pm
- Season: Inside year round Outside May-October
- A Preferred Wedding Services list is available.
- Music: audio - sound levels monitored
- Alcohol: Charles Krug wine only,
  champagne permitted and keg beers
  which must be served by the caterer. No hard liquor
- Parking: ample
- Services: tables, chairs, bbq, minimal kitchen, set-up, clean-up
- Deposits: $500 to secure the date
- Fees: $30. per person with a $1,500 minimum for one space.
  $ 5. more per person with $1750 minimum for both spaces.
- Insurance: additional liability required.

Phone: 707-967-2245 Melanie Mooers • 707-967-2243 Nicki Simon
Winery: 707-963-5057 + toll free 888-ASK-KRUG
Fax: 707-967-2294
Internet
E mail: specialevents@pmondavi.com
Shown by appointment only.
Address: 2800 St. Helena Hwy., St. Helena, CA 94574

1 hour from the Golden Gate Bridge. A map is needed for your guests. Your guests may stay at Meadowood Resort, Harvest Inn, Inn at Southbridge and Bartels Ranch. Rehearsal dinners may be held at Pinot Blanc, Trilogy, Restaurant at Greystone, Ristorante Tra Vigne

- See the Day Trips section of this book for fun things to do while in the area.

BISTRO DON GIOVANNI
NAPA ~ NAPA COUNTY

The Scala's, Donna and Giovanni, have designed a true "Italian Bistro". The fireplace both inside and out create a warm atmosphere along with the beautiful vegetable and herb gardens. The cuisine is regional Italian and country French.

The restaurant has high ratings in the valley for Donna Scala's wonderful recipes. Cathy Cora is the other chef who rounds out the excellent menu for this established location. Their wine list reads like the "Who's Who" of Napa. Though wines are predominant here, the bartender is quite capable of many specialty drinks.

They will provide a reception for 80 guests, but it must be on Sunday nights or mid-week.

Elopments and "Special Touches" to romantic dinners are part of the skills offered here, as well as Celebrations!

LOCATION ACCOMMODATES

- Receptions and Rehearsal Dinners
- 80 guests
- Season: Patio - April through October
- Music: monitored
- Alcohol: wines and hard liquor
- Parking: ample
- Deposit: to reserve date
- Fees: upon request

Phone: 707-224-3300
Address: 4110 St. Helena Highway, Napa, Ca 94558

Forty minutes from the Golden Gate Bridge
A map is needed for your guests
Your guests may stay at the John Muir Inn,
La Residence Country Inn, Silverado Country Club

LARKMEAD COUNTRY INN
CALISTOGA ~ NAPA COUNTY

Larkmead Country Inn is both a wonderful wedding and reception location and an enjoyable honeymoon spot. Nestled in the vineyards along the Napa River the historic California Victorian country home welcomes you with verandas, grassy lawns and a canopy of ancient oak and sycamore trees to shade you from the warm sun. The fieldstone wall with vineyards beyond are an excellent backdrop for photographs. The ancient magnolia trees bloom in June.

Large events are spring through autumn with lawn weddings and reception parties. Smaller ceremonies may be held indoors by the fireplace or on the veranda. For larger groups the Inn is closed to other guests so you may have a private event.

This is an excellent setting for a retreat wedding, so the families may get to know one another, or an elopement providing you with a honeymoon location central to the beautiful Napa Valley.

The historic home is furbished with Persian carpets, antiques, fine old paintings and prints which were collected over the years. Each of the bedrooms is named for a wine. Spacious, light and airy with the added plus of overlooking the vineyards.

The continental breakfast is served daily to guests in the dining room or on the porches in the warmer months.

LOCATION ACCOMMODATES

- Weddings - Receptions
- Elopements - Retreat Weddings - Out of town guests
- Indoors - 2 to 10 for fireplace ceremonies
- Outdoors -150 seated guests
- Season - outdoor from May through October, indoor throughout the year
- Preferred Caterer and Coordinator Teri Piper Johnson
- Preferred Wedding Services list is available.
- Music: sound levels - monitored
- Alcohol: through caterer
- Parking: limited, valet for large groups
- Deposits: upon reserving date
- Fees: upon request
- Insurance:

Phone: 707-942-5432 for caterer and coordinator
Phone: Honeymoon or guests 707-942-5360
Internet:
E mail:
Address: 1103 Larkmead Lane, Calistoga, CA 94515

90 minutes from the Golden Gate Bridge. A map is needed for your guests. Your guests may stay at Falcon's Nest, Oliver House, Comfort Inn, Christopher's Inn, or Indian Springs. Rehearsal dinners may be planned next door at the Larkmead Kornell Cellars (they create excellent Champagne), Calistoga Inn Restaurant with the Napa Valley Brewery Co. or All Seasons Cafe and nearby Meadowood Grill.

- See the Day Trips section of this book for fun things to do while in the area.

RESTAURANTE TRA VIGNE
ST. HELENA ~ NAPA COUNTY

A small vineyard grows outside the eight-foot high fieldstone walls which hide a shaded courtyard at the well-known Tra Vigne Restaurant in St. Helena. The restored winery is known among the locals as "the meeting place" for a drink, lunch or dinner. What many do not know is they also offer their talents and experience in creating lovely receptions and rehearsal dinners.

The chef and staff offer only the finest and freshest foods. The restaurant is owned by the same group who brought us Mustards, Fog City, Roti and the Buckeye Roadhouse. Foods are served with a presentation known to our region and becoming famous world-wide. The wine list and full bar compliment beautiful foods and detailed service. Details of your event are overseen by David Yoshida.

LOCATION ACCOMMODATES

- Receptions and Rehearsal Dinners only
- Indoor Banquet Room - 64 guests - year round
- Outdoor Courtyard - 120 guests - summers at 11 a.m.
- Music: no amplified music and no dancing
- Alcohol: full bar and wine list
- Parking: limited
- Deposits: to reserve date
- Fees: upon request

Phone: 707-963-4449, David Yoshida, Special Event Coordinator,
        Kellie Wilson, Associate
E mail: 103064,476
Address: 1050 Charter Oak Avenue, St. Helena, CA 94574

One hour from Golden Gate Bridge. A map is needed for your guests. Your guests may stay at the La Fleur B&B, Harvest Inn, Meadowood Resort or the Wine Country Inn. Rehearsal Dinners in St. Helena, may be held on site, Showleys and Tarra.

SEQUOIA GROVE
NAPA ~ NAPA COUNTY

PHOTO BY LIGHTWORKS

Sequoia Grove's barn, lawns and home nestle beneath the giant hundred year old sequoia trees - one of the last stands in the Napa Valley. They provide shade for hearty celebrations as families gather and friends share special, loving moments with couples being wed.

A rustic barn is the tasting room. Nearby bbq's, patio and grassy areas with surrounding vineyards give this location a warm, homey feeling. The Allen Family Winery provides the lawns and colorful gardens, then leaves the rest to festive families who may use the site throughout the day and early evening for weddings and receptions. There is room for a tent to be added in case of changeable weather.

The award winning wines produced by this 24 acre estate consist of Cabernet Sauvignon, Chardonnay, Merlot, Petit Verdot. In 1988 the winery was named Winery of the Year by International Wine Review. The Allen family offers you their wines at a excellent discount for your event.

The century old winery sports the only under-ground wine celler in Napa Valley. This cellar keeps wine barrels at an even 55 degrees fahrenheit and constant humidity year round. The 1860 barn and tasting room houses eighteen upright oak tanks which are an eyeful for any visitor.

PHOTO BY LIGHTWORKS

LOCATION ACCOMMODATES

• Weddings - Receptions
• Tasting and Cask room - 40 guests
• Outdoor - 150 guests
• Seasonal: May through October
• Time: 10:am - 11:30pm
• A Preferred Wedding Services list available.
• Music: sound levels - monitored
• Alcohol: Sequoia Grove Wines only.
• Parking: limited
• Deposit: $625
• Fees: Packet upon request
• Insurance: Additional certificate of liability requested.

Phone: 707-944-2945
Fax: 707-963-9411
Internet
E Mail
Address: 8338 St. Helena Highway, Napa, CA 94558

Your Guests may stay at The Inn at Southbridge, The Ink House, The Zinfandel Inn, The Harvest Inn Embassy Suites in Napa, Best Western Inn in Napa. Rehearsal Dinners at Napa Valley Wine Train, Pinot Blanc in St. Helena and Piatti.

• See the Day Trips section of this book for fun things to do while in the area.

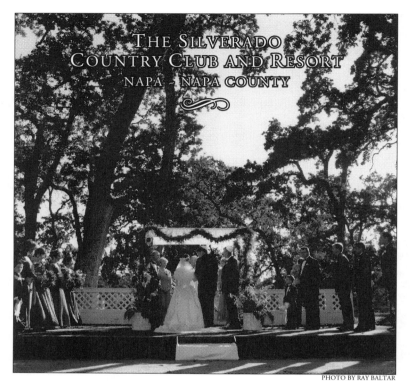

When standards are high, Silverado meets everyone's expectations. This beautiful country club and resort has every amenity to offer a couple whether they are being married in the lovely settings or spending their honeymoon, or both.

The plantation-style country club houses many different restaurants and banquet rooms. Excellent menus are created specifically for your event by the catering department. Whether you choose a romantic dinner for two, a rehearsal dinner for forty or a gala wedding reception for 500 the chefs and staff work toward making your occasion a perfect and happy one.

There are several outdoor dining areas in a variety of settings; from redwoods and arbors to lovely golf course greens. Their grand ballroom with crystal chandeliers will seat 450. The outside locations will expand to

500 guests at The Grove. Ponds, lakes and bridges with a mountain backdrop are all part of the beauty on these 360 acres.

The original land grant from General Vallejo was given to his brother Salvador and called Rancho Yajome. Later acquired by General John Miller, the great mansion was constructed in 1870. Many generals and President Theodore Roosevelt stayed in its beautiful rooms.

Bringing a family or retreat wedding to this location is pure enjoyment. The location affords jogging trails, tennis courts, and two 18 hole Robert Trent Jones Golf Courses, 8 swimming pools and first-rate accommodations. Their 280 suites include kitchen, fireplace, living and dining room, romantic bedrooms with private patio or deck.

PHOTO BY RAY BALTAR

LOCATION ACCOMMODATES

- Weddings and Receptions
- Honeymoons and Elopements
- Indoor and Outdoor Locations
- Events from five to 500 guests
- Season: year round
- Time: varies
- A Preferred Wedding Services list is available
- Music: monitored
- Alcohol: full bar and Napa Valley Wines
- Parking: ample
- Deposits: upon booking of location
- Fees: upon request

Phone: 707-257-0200 - Catering, Events
Fax: 707-257-5407
Internet: www.silveradoresort.com
E mail: off the web page
Address: 1600 Atlas Peak Rd., Napa, CA 94558

60 minutes from the Golden Gate Bridge. A map is needed for your guests. Your guests may stay at Silverado. Rehearsal dinners at Silverado.

STERLING VINEYARDS
CALISTOGA ~ NAPA COUNTY

The distant view of Sterling reminds one of a walled city somewhere in the Mediterranean holy lands. Built to be an extraordinary winery and tasting facility this winery lends its setting to wonderful events. Events may be planned at the Winery Lake Plaza, Sterling View Terrace or elegant Visitors Center, Three Palms Room and Patio or the Diamond Mountain Ranch Veranda. The views of nearby mountains and vineyards are the most dramatic in the valley. Events combine several areas and foods are served inside.

Your guests, if need be, may be driven up the hill. The exciting arrival and part of the fun is to ride the aerial tramway which takes you gliding across the top of the trees and into the white walled winery tiled entry. Summer and early autumn ceremonies often include warm evenings and sunsets for your reception.

Winery staff pour the excellent Chardonnay, Merlot, and Cabernet Reserve and Diamond Mountain Cabernet plus Cabernet Sauvignon for your guests. The winery is now owned by Seagram Corporation.

LOCATION ACCOMMODATES

- Weddings and Receptions
- 200 guests maximum
- Season: Outdoor - April through Early November
- Inside Season: year round - 50 guests minimum
- Time Allowed: 6 hour maximum
- Set-up 5:30pm
- Ceremonies and receptions 6:30pm - 11:pm
- Consultant from selected list - required
- Preferred Wedding Services list available
- Kitchen: available for caterer
- Tables/Chairs and Glassware - provided
- Music: sound levels monitored
- Alcohol: Sterling selections
- Parking: ample
- Deposits: 50% of the total location fee (non-refundable unless re-booked)
- Insurance: Certificate of Insurance required

Phone: 707-942-5432, to view or reserve the property.
Fax:
Internet Number
E mail
Address: 1111 Dunaweal Lane , Calistoga, CA 94515

90 minutes from Golden Gate Bridge on St. Helena Highway (29) North. A map is needed for your guests.

Your guests may stay at Meadowood Resort, Calistoga Inn, Wine Way Inn, The Elms, and Christopher's Inn Rehearsal dinners may be held at All Seasons Cafe, Pacifico Catahoula Restaurant in Calistoga, or Brava Terrace in St.Helena

- See the Day Trips Section of this book for fun things to do while in the area.

St. Supery Vineyards and Winery
RUTHERFORD ~ NAPA COUNTY

St. Suprey offers two beautiful and distinct settings for your wedding and reception. Nestled in the vineyards along Hwy. 29 in Rutherford, the site reflects the old and new with the elegant 1882 Queen Anne Victorian, (available for portraits and bridal dressing), as well as, the modern structure of the wine gallery and museum. Beautiful outdoor areas are available with oak trees, gardens and lawns to set your tables against the vineyard backdrop.

The windowed second-story gallery of the winery looks out over hundreds of acres of vineyards and toward the distant mountains on both sides of the wide valley. Late September through early November affords exceptional vineyard views of autumn colors across the valley.

Your guests will gain knowledge about grape varieties, soils and local artists display in the

PHOTO BY CREATIVE FOCUS

gallery. It houses local artists' works and a unique self-tour winery museum offers information pertinent to wine tasting and aromas.

The award winning wines available for your event are Chardonnay, Sauvignon Blanc, and Cabernet Sauvignon.

The on-site event consultants will go over details of the preferred list of vendors and the winery procedure. Because of their concern and support of your wedding and reception, it will be a smooth flowing event. The location will also host rehearsal dinners and bridal luncheons and offers private group tours for your wedding guests.

PHOTO BY MARGRETHA LANE

LOCATION ACCOMMODATES

- Weddings and Receptions
- Indoor gallery - 120 or 350 guest-standing
- Season - year round
- Minimum guests - 60 guests or $1500 minimum fee.
- Time: Events may begin and end: 5:30 to 10:30 pm
- Preferred Wedding Services list is available
- Alcohol - St. Supery selections

- Outdoor lawns - 300 guests
- Music - sound levels-monitored
- Parking - ample and convenient

60 minutes from Golden Gate Bridge
Deposits: $300 non-refundable
Fees: upon request

Phone: 707-963-4507 - Wedding Consultants
Fax: 707-963-4526
Internet Number: http//www.STSUPERY.COM
E mail: DIVINECAB@AOL.COM
Address: 8440 St. Helena Hwy. Rutherford, CA 94573

A map is needed for your guests. Your guests may stay at Meadowood Hotel, Wine Country Inn, Rustridge Ranch B&B, The Chateau, The Farmhouse B&B. Rehearsal dinners may be planned on site or on the Wine Train, Auberge du Soleil, Pinoit Blanc, The Culinary Institute of America at Greystone, Freemark Abbey, Showleys, The Restaurant or Grill at Meadowood Resort.

- See the Day Trips Section of this book for fun things to do while in the area.

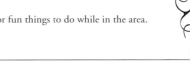

V. SATTUI WINERY
ST. HELENA ~ NAPA COUNTY

Four generations of the family-owned winery have continued a hundred year tradition - hospitality and excellent wines. A favorite spot amongst the locals for years as one of the greatest picnic spots, excellent winery, deli and gift store. The Sattui family added an beautiful event location for continued celebrations of life.

PHOTO BY SATTUI

The new winery and event building reflect "old world charm". The designer and stone masons built hand-hewn stone walls with touches of wrought iron. The balconies and decks are of heavy rustic timbers to balance the strength of the stone building. Restful tri-level terraces and a fountain are shaded by majestic 200 year old oak trees. Spacious gardens and acres of lawns and vineyards frame the lovely castle-like building.

The oak barrels number 1000 in the subterranean wine cellar. You and your guests will feel like royalty as you are seated for dinner in the romantically lit atmosphere. Beautiful intimate ceremonies may be performed in a smaller aromatic wine cellar amongst the oak barrels. The private cellar holds 32 guests and provides a venue for small weddings or rehearsal dinners.

V. Sattui produces a top Johannasberg Reisling. Sweet wines are Muscat, Camay, Medea. Cabernet and Sauvignons in several varieties are available for your guests.

The small patio and lawn in front of the tower area are a wonderful backdrop for the outdoor ceremony and photographs.

LOCATION ACCOMMODATES

- Weddings and Receptions
- Elopements
- Indoor - Subterranean Cellar w/ 1000 oak wine barrels - 250 guests
- Indoor - Private Cellar will seat 32 guests
- Outdoor -Tri-level Terrace & Courtyard - 250 guests
- Season: year round
- Time: 6:pm to 11:pm
- Preferred Wedding Services list available.
- Music: sound levels monitored
- Alcohol: V. Sattui - selections - case discounts, beer
- No corkage fees for V.Sattui wines.
- Tables and chairs provided - rounds for 200 guests
- Party Rental services needed.
- Parking: ample
- Date Reservation: $200. non-refundable
- Deposits: 50% deposit non-refundable
- Fees are $25.00 per person- Saturdays minimum of 100
  1750 Flat Rate all other evenings
- Insurance: additionally insured policy required.

Phone: 707-963-7774 x 101 - Kelly Allgyer Hospitality Director
Fax: 707-963-5745
E mail: kallgyer@aol.com
Address: 1111 White Lane at Hwy. 29, St. Helena, CA 94574

60 minutes from Golden Gate Bridge. A map to area is suggested for your guests. Your guests may stay at The Inn at Southbridge, LaFleur B&B, Harvest Inn, El Bonita Motel, Hotel St. Helena, White Sulphur Springs Resort, and Meadowood Resort Hotel. Rehearsal dinners may be planned at Terra, Greystone Brava Terrace, Ristorante Tra Vigne or Pairs Cafe.

- See the Day Trips Section of this book for fun things to do while in the area.

Yountville Community Hall
Yountville ~ Napa County

This affordable hall will give you an understanding of how former valley residents met and celebrated in a community atmosphere. For many years the well-maintained building has been the location fo town meetings, youth activities and celebrations of life. The building is adjacent to the vineyards and within view of the Vintage 1870 buildings in the little town of Yountville.

The large hall has a stage, hardwood floors and a full kitchen which allows family or most caterers in the area to provide for celebrations. There are two smaller side rooms to use for a variety of reasons. You are able to plan an inside/outside event here. Ceremonies are often held on the back lawn. It has been a favorite location for local people for many years.

Recent additions have been the patio area at the rear of the building, a bbq area and flower gardens. New shade trees have been planted around the patio area.

Nearby is a church ceremony area. photo of It is called The Little Church In The Vale. The Yountville Community Church is a half-mile from the reception hall. It is a delight to any who use this historic 1874 building. The church is open to the public and they love doing weddings. It has a delightful steeple and chimes, and of course, it is picture perfect.

LOCATION ACCOMMODATES

• Weddings and Receptions
• Hall: 250 seated - guests
• Season: Year round
• Music: audio - monitored for sound levels
• Alcohol: permitted
• Parking: parking lot plus adjacent site
• Deposits: 25%
• Insurance: personal liability insurance required

Yountville Community Hall
Phone: 707-944-2959 Skip Walters
Internet: http://www.napanet.net
E mail:
Address: 6516 Yount Street, Yountville, CA 94599

Yountville Community Church 707-944-2179
Little Church In The Vale
6621 Yount Street, Yountville, CA 94599

40 minutes from the Golden Gate Bridge. A map is needed for your guests. Your guests may stay at Webber House B&B, Napa Valley Lodge, Vintage Inn or Bordeaux House.

Rehearsal dinners may be held at Domaine Chandon, Piatti, Stars Oakville Cafe or Rutherford Grill, Hopper Creek, Napa Valley Grill.

BARTHOLOMEW PARK WINERY
SONOMA ~ SONOMA COUNTY

Driving the winding lanes to Bartholomew Park Winery is a rewarding experience. Eucalyptus, oak trees, and 400 acres of rolling hills covered with vineyards in all directions greet you and your guests as they arrive for your wedding, reception or party.

The historical 75 year-old Winery building surrounded by oaks and vineyards gives the impression of a historic chapel or monastery by its Spanish Colonial style. Ceremonies and receptions may be held in the rustic, yet comfortable interior of this building, outside in a natural Oak Grove, in the more formal Wine Garden, or above the Garden on the Celtic Circle. Deemed "the most romantic, as well as the most historic destination in the Wine Country..." by the San Francisco Chronicle, this vineyard setting is perfectly romantic for photographs. Flowers and natural grasses give visual appeal to this hillside vineyard setting.

PHOTO BY BARTHOLOMEW

Bartholomew Park wines are sold exclusively at the winery. They specialize in five vineyard designated varietals: Chardonnay, Pinot Noir, Merlot, Cabernet Sauvignon and Zinfindel. These 1830 vineyards are considered to be some of the oldest in California.

The wines are available for your guests for the celebration. The winery staff will help you select a caterer from their qualified list and guide you through the process of planning a memorable wedding.

PHOTO BY BARTHOLOMEW

LOCATION ACCOMMODATES

- Weddings, Receptions or parties
- Inside - 40-100 guests
- Outside - 60-120 guests
- Season: year round.
- Preferred Wedding Services List Available.
- Ample parking
- Alcohol: Bartholomew Park selections and sparkling wine available from Gloria Ferrer. Any other choice of wines will incurr a $10. corkage fee.
- Music: is monitored. Amplified music -inside only.
- Time: 6:30 pm to 10:30 pm, set-up at 5:pm
- Limited kitchen, water and power is available.
- Deposits and Fees: information upon request

Phone: Tasting Room, 707-935-9511
Fax: 707-935-0549
Internet Number
E mail
Address: 1000 Vineyard Lane, Sonoma, CA 95476

A map is needed for your guests. 50 minutes from the Golden Gate Bridge off Hwy 12 Guests may stay in nearby Sonoma at the El Dorado, Sonoma Hotel, Sonoma Mission Inn, Realis du Soleil B&B Rehearsal dinners may be held at the winery itself, The General's Daughter and Piatti Restaurants, Swiss Hotel or Della Santina's

*See the Day Trips Section of this book for fun things guests and honeymooners may do while in the area.

THE BELTANE RANCH
GLEN ELLEN ~ SONOMA COUNTY

The historic Beltane Ranch has been a bed and breakfast for many years providing guests beautiful memories of gently rolling vineyard hillsides backdropped against the dynamic Mayacmus Mountain range - the center of the Valley of the Moon which Jack London made famous with his home.

Owner Rosemary Wood relayed a marvelous story of the original bunkhouse and several ranch owners from 1892 to present. She decided to change it into a bed and breakfast and expressed that she and her daughter now believe it would give many a future bride and her guests a happy wedding celebration location. The entire site is reserved over the weekend for the couple to enjoy with family or friends during the

wedding celebration. Five guest rooms, tennis court, personal library, eight miles of hiking trails and some of the best wineries in the nation are at your fingertips.

Intimate weddings or elopements are lovely year round in front of the massive fireplace. Large outdoor events for 300 guests are held under the hundred year old oaks. A nearby barn, verandas, rose and flower gardens, plus miles of vineyards and rock walls comprise views most people only see in photos. An excellent choice for a romantic honeymoon spot.

LOCATION ACCOMMODATES

• Weddings, Receptions and Elopements
• Retreat Weddings and Honeymoons
• maximum 300
• Season: outdoor - May to mid October
• Inside: year round - 20 maximum
• Time: all day events possible
• Preferred Wedding Services list is available
• Music: sound levels monitored
• Party Rental required for tables and chairs
• Parking: provided pasture area
• Deposits: upon request
• Fees: upon request
• Insurance: Required

Phone: 707-833-4233
Fax: 707-833-4233
P.O. Box 1217
Address: 11775 Sonoma Hwy., Glen Ellen, CA 95442

A map is needed for your guests. Your guests may stay at Relais du Soleil B&B, Gaige House B&B, Sonoma Hotel, Swiss Hotel, El Dorado Hotel and the Thistle Dew Inn. Rehearsal dinners may be held at the Depot Restaurant, The Generals Daughter, Kunde Winery Caves (with caterer).

• See the Day Trips Section of this book for fun things to do while in the area.

BUENA VISTA WINERY
SONOMA ~ SONOMA COUNTY

The vine covered walls hold years of stories about the wonderful celebrations, symphonies and events enjoyed in this lovely setting. Buena Vista - beautiful view is a correct name for this historic winery. The fieldstone building looks out over vineyards dating back to 1857 when Count Agoston Haraszthy brought the first wine stock to the area and planted it in the rich Sonoma soil. The vineyards have grown to a thousand acres.

Ceremonies are held early evening in the fountain courtyard with a historic fieldstone building in the background. Planted with flowers, the courtyard ambiance is one of peace and tranquility under the fragrant eucalyptus trees and oaks.

The wine tasting and event room is where receptions are held. The wine racks and exceptionally long bar add to the exposed stone wall's European castle-like appearance. The exposed stone walls and heavy wooden beams lend the rustic winery look many brides look for. The rich long bar is across one entire wall of the room. A massive fireplace warms the room throughout the cooler seasons. James Patrick has accomplished elegant events in this lovely room. It is possible to hold a smaller ceremony in front of the fireplace.

Your guests may take the self-guided tour, dance, enjoy the art gallery and sip the wines you choose to serve. The Buena Vista Winery has been a top award winner with their blends of Chardonnays, Merlot, Zinfandel, Gewurztraminer and Pinot Noir and many other excellent choices.

LOCATION ACCOMMODATES

- Weddings and Receptions minimum 40
- Outdoor ceremony area - 100 guests, 100 seated
- Inside reception area - 120 guests, 200 standing
- Season: year round for indoor
- Time: 6:30 pm to 10:30 pm (evening lighting)
- A Preferred Wedding Services list is available.
- No Caterer's kitchen - power and water available.
- Music: sound levels monitored - outside dance floor
- Alcohol: Buena Vista Wines
- Parking: ample
- Deposits: to reserve the date
- Fees: upon request of packet. Fees include set-up, clean-up, staff and tables/chairs
- Insurance:

Phone: 800-926-1266 or 707-938-1266
Fax: 707-939-0916
Internet:
E mail:
Address: 18000 Old Winery Road, Sonoma, CA 95476

Forty-five minutes from the Golden Gate Bridge. A map is needed for your guests. Your guests may stay at the Sonoma Hotel, El Dorado Hotel or Thistle Dew Inn. Rehearsal dinners may be held at Piatti, The Generals Daughter, La Casa or Zinos on the Plaza.

- See the Day Trips section of this book for fun things to do while in the area.

B.R. COHN WINERY
GLEN ELLEN ~ SONOMA COUNTY

B.R. Cohn Winery is situated on a lovely hillside in an olive grove along Hwy. 12 between Sonoma and Kenwood. The location has a beautiful ceremony and event sites and picnic areas near the working ranch buildings, tasting room terrace or a romantic spot called "The theater in the vines," appropriately named because of the stunning backdrop of hillside vineyards.

PHOTO BY RAY BALTAR

The oak covered rugged western range of Sonoma Mountains are in the distance. There are no blocked views for your guests during the ceremony as they are seated amphitheater style on a nearby hillside, or for smaller weddings on the ceremony deck. A road gives ease to moving ambulatory or elderly to the area and gives a picturesque path for a horse drawn carriage.

Seeing this spot in the spring and summer is magnificent, but the autumn shades are glorious. Ceremonies being held on this creekside deck give way later to music, dancing, or serving your

PHOTO BY RAY BALTAR

feast. The wedding design may be elegant or casual but always beautiful and memorable in these surroundings. An exceptional location.

Other available areas are the large grassy area near the tasting room. This is perfect for serving dinner. There is great versatility to this location.

The rock n roll Doobie Brother's manager now owns B.R. Cohn Winery. He began his vintage releases in 1984. The winery makes Cabernet, Chardonnays, plus Merlot and Pinot Noir for you and your guests to enjoy while there.

PHOTO BY RAY BALTAR

LOCATION ACCOMMODATES

- Weddings and Receptions
- Outdoor: 100 to 300 guests
- Season: early May through October.
- Preferred Wedding Services List Available.
- Alcohol: B.R. Cohn only.
- Parking: Ample
- Music: Sound monitored outdoors.
- Time:
- Fees and Deposits: Upon request.

Phone: 707-938-4064 - Site Event Coordinator
Fax: 707-938-4585
Internet Number: http://www.weddinglinks.com/
E mail
Address: 15140 Sonoma Hwy., Glen Ellen, CA

A map is needed for your guests. 60 minutes from San Francisco off Hwy. 12

Guests may stay at nearby Sonoma Mission Inn, Jack London Lodge, Gaige House, or Realis du Soleil B&B Rehearsal Dinners are possible at Piatte, Sonoma Mission Inn, and nearby Kenwood Restaurant.

- See the Day Trips Section of book for fun things to do in the area while visiting.

CLINE CELLARS
SONOMA ~ SONOMA COUNTY

If you are planning a large event this is one of the largest sites available. The exceptionally beautiful setting of oak covered hills, miles of vineyards, ponds, decks, and rock walls with over 5,000 roses bushes lends a casual elegance to any wedding and reception. Full moons are extraodinary in this location.

The 1850 farmhouse is now the Tasting Room. There are a variety of locations for ceremonies and/or receptions on the site whether you need an indoor or outdoor event. Intimate parties of 10 or large events up to 1,000 guests are welcome.

The family operated winery is situated on a previous Miwok Indian site in the Carneros region along Hwy. 121 in the Sonoma Valley. They have re-created a mission chapel area for ceremonies up to 60. A vintage rail car and deck overlooking several duck ponds and vineyards which is a unique setting for 140 guests. The Barrel Room is available for indoor events up to 500 seated. The lawns allow for 1,000 guests. A special festival tent with cathedral windows is available for 125 seated guests.

The wines available from the Cline brothers are earning an excellent reputation. The Zinfandel and Rhone style Varietals are from their vineyards in Contra Costa. The bountiful Merlot, and speciality wines are grown on Sonoma Counties lovely properties. They make their wines available for events at a 25% discount.

The characteristics and visual dynamics of this site are a photographer's pleasure. The site's numerous venues offer something for everyone, from wine estate elegance to historical California in themes.

LOCATION ACCOMMODATES

- Weddings and Receptions: 10 to 1,000 guests
- Indoor Barrel Room - 500 guests, seated
- Indoor Barrel Room - 700 guests, standing
- Vintage Rail Car and Deck - 110 guests
- Tasting Room Verandah - 32 guests
- Preferred Wedding Services List available
- Alcohol: Cline Cellars selections
- Festival Tent: 125 - seated to 170 - standing
- Time: Begin any time throughout the day. 5 hour event

- Mission Chapel & Patio - 120 guests
- Season: year round
- Great Lawn - 1,000 guests
- Music: sound levels monitored
- Parking: ample parking available.

Deposits: $500 Security Deposit
Fees: Base fee $20.per person, includes wine glasses, bar & server.
         Tables, cloths & chairs. Event Coordinator
Insurance: Additionally insured policy required

Phone: 707-935-4310 - Special Events
Fax: 707-935-4319
Internet Number: clinecellars.com
E mail: epcline@sonic.net
Address: 24737 Arnold Drive, Sonoma, CA 95476

An easy 35 minutes from the Golden Gate Bridge. A map is available for your guests. Your guests will love staying in Sonoma at the Sonoma Hotel, Thistle Dew Inn, El Dorado Hotel and Sonoma Valley Inn. Rehearsal dinners may be planned on site or at any of the fine restaurants in Sonoma.

- See the Day Trips Section of this book for fun things to do while in the area.

THE FARMHOUSE INN AND RESTAURANT
FORESTVILLE ~ SONOMA COUNTY

PHOTO BY FARMHOUSE

Within view of the vineyards in the beautiful Russian River Valley stands the charming turn-of-the-century Farmhouse Inn. This handsome farmhouse with porch shaded by huge oaks sits amongst well tended gardens. The back deck is also shaded by oaks and connects to the lovely poolside gardens.

This is an excellent "retreat wedding atmosphere" where you and your families may get to know one another preceding the event. Your guest list can swell to 250 the day of your event.

The Farmhouse Inn has eight cottages set on six wooded acres for up to twenty overnight guests. The Inn is decorated in antiques of the period and all guest rooms are designed in a English cottage atmosphere. Several cottages have fireplaces, jacuzzi tubs and saunas. You and your overnight guests may enjoy the swimming pool which is adjacent to the gardens.

The exceptional, award-winning restaurant prepares a full country breakfast each morning for guests. The staff will work with you to create the perfect menu for your wedding and reception guests. Menus are designed to your taste and served with style in this romantic and relaxed atmosphere.

In 1997 the Farmhouse Inn has plans to build a separate event center. "The Barn" at the Farmhouse Inn overlooks the pool and has been designed to provide additional space for weddings and events.

Honeymooners are treated special here. They are fed and left alone to enjoy one another…..if that is what they choose. The property allows for privacy. The Farmhouse Inn is central to the Russian River area and a quick drive to Healdsburg, or Santa Rosa for some night life.

PHOTO BY FARMHOUSE

LOCATION ACCOMMODATES

- Weddings - Receptions - Elopements - Honeymoons
- Gardens and Inn 300 guests
- The Barn 125 guests
- Indoor and Outdoor Events
- Season: year round events.
- Time available: morning through evening.
- Music: Sound levels monitored.
- A Preferred Wedding Service List is available
- Caterer: in/house caterer
- Parking: for up to 100 guests.
- Alcohol: wine and beer served from the bar. Corking fee for outside beverages.
- Deposits: required to reserve date
- Fees: packet upon request
- Insurance:

Rebecca Smith, Event Coordinator
Phone: 707-887-3300 or 800-464-6642
Fax: 707-887-3311
Email: innkeep@sonic.net
Internet Number: http://www.sonic.net/farmhouse
Address: 7871 River Road, Forestville, CA 95436

90 minutes from the Golden Gate Bridge. A map is suggested for your guests. Your guests may stay nearby at Raford House B&B, or in Santa Rosa at Fountain Grove Inn, Los Robles Lodge or The Hilton Hotel. Rehearsal dinners may be planned at the hotels above, Ca Bianca, Cazanoma Lodge or Chez Peyo.

- See the Day Trips section of this book for fun things to do while in the area.

GABRIELLE'S VINEYARD
SANTA ROSA ~ SONOMA COUNTY

The neo-Victorian home looks out over one of the prettiest valleys of vineyards in the hills near Santa Rosa. The home was designed by Donald A. Gardener. Tho new, the home represents a picturesque era and offers a very modern and complete event location. The twenty-five acre vineyard has been planted to the lay of the land leaving the lovely stands of oaks to provide several secluded spots for outdoor ceremonies. The views include the young Merlot vines which are planted on 15 acres of the property.

Inside, gleaming hardwood floors, windows, and a beautiful fireplace extends hospitality to the couple and their guests. French doors open onto the deck which covers the entire back of the house. From the deck you step onto a lovely lawn with a trellised arbor for ceremonies. Rose gardens and a small pond add charm to the location. It is not uncommon for the owners to awaken to deer nearby, nibbling the roses and drinking from the pond. The privacy, food and enviroment this location affords make it an exceptional location.

The location accents the beauty of our California golden hills in the summer. As the vineyard grows and turns autumn hues by October it makes this an entirely different setting.

Gabrielle brings her organizational and catering talents to this exceptional private location. Making every event a special occasion is a skill she has achieved through the years as a professional.

PHOTO BY GABRIELLE

LOCATION ACCOMMODATES

- Weddings - Receptions
- Elopements - Rehearsal Dinners
- Indoor/Outdoor - 175 guests
- Indoor - 75 guests
- Season: April through October
- Time: inquire
- In-House catering by Gabrielle
- A preferred Wedding Services list is available.
- Music: sound levels monitored.
- Alcohol: may be ordered through caterer
- Parking: 80 car limit
- Deposits: 50% to reserve location.
- Fees: upon request
- Insurance: liability insurance required

Phone: 707-527-6771, Caterer, Gabrielle Ridgeway
Internet
E mail:
Address: by appointment

60 minutes from the Golden Gate Bridge. A map is needed for your guests. Your guests may stay Red Lion in Rohnert Park, The Flamingo Hotel or The Gables B&B. Rehearsal dinners may be held at LaGrande Trattoria Restaurant, Flamingo and Red Lion Hotels, CaBianca or Mixx in Santa Rosa.

- See the Day Trips section of this book for fun things to do while in this area.

THE GARDENS AT KENWOOD FARMS
KENWOOD ~ SONOMA COUNTY

This unusual property is a different type of setting for a wedding. Perfect for Western themes with a barn nearby and wagons of various types on the property. Yet, the site provides an elegant setting with the lawns and the awe inspiring views plus elegant tent. The remarkable location gains everyone's response to relax and have fun. It is bordered by distant vineyards and a strawberry farm. The landscaping and gardens include a wedding arbor, pond and fountain. The owners have a lovely large tent for events. The big plus is the rustic barn which was converted to a dance area and wet bar. This has a covered and shaded terrace.

Standing in this part of the Valley of the Moon you may look straight up to Sugar Loaf Ridge, a part of the Maycaymus ridge. Large oaks and newly planted trees shade the expansive lawns. Virginia Donham and John Frediani have long shared the dream to develop this lovely land and bring together celebrations of life. They were determined it should be different, and it is.

The property has a tiny cottage with a rail-post around the porch. This houses the bride as she and her attendants ready themselves for the ceremony. Truly a great photographic spot. The grounds have a winter creek and fish pond with fountain. Several rustic wagons loaded with flowers and eye appeal are part of the scenery.

LOCATION ACCOMMODATES

- Weddings - Receptions • Retreat and Theme Events
- Outdoor events only • 25 - 350 - guests
- Season: April through October
- Time: 6 hours plus 2 hrs prior to event
- Music: sound levels monitored
- Caterers: most outside caterers acceptable have caterer and co-ordinator available
- Rentals: tables and chairs on site.
- Alcohol: wine beer champagne - no corkage fee
- Parking: off street parking available
- Deposits: upon date reservation
- Fees: upon request
- Insurance:

Phone: 707-833-5611
Fax:
Internet:
E mail:
Address: 9250 A Sonoma Hwy 12, Kenwood, CA

60 minutes from the Golden Gate Bridge. A map is needed for your guests. Your guests may stay at the Gaige House, Beltane B&B, Creekside Inn-Santa Rosa. Rehearsal dinners at the Sonoma Mission Inn, Kenwood Resturant, Cafe Citti patio or Flamingo Hotel

- See the Day Trips section of this book for fun things to do while in this area.

VALLEJO'S HOME AND GARDEN
SONOMA ~ SONOMA COUNTY

PHOTO BY MATT KENNEALLY

A long lane of towering trees leads you to a historic state park dedicated to Vallejo's history. The permanent home and garden of General Mariano Vallejo, the first Mexican Commandant and his family, is available for wedding ceremonies. The beautiful setting in the casual flower garden sits under huge oaks and other lovely shade trees. The gardens surround a delightful Victorian house and museum.

Lachryma Montis, "tears of the mountain", is a delightful two-story Gothic revival home. It was built in 1852 from a pre-fabricated frame home and shipped around the horn of South America, then brought into Sonoma. This delightful home has ornate windows, gables and fencing. A picture perfect backdrop for your wedding.

PHOTO BY MATT KENNEALLY

A small vineyard has grown just outside the picket fence for years. Nearby in the garden is a tiny building called the El Delirio. Ceremonies are often held here, or several other areas work beautifully. In Spring the climbing roses mantel the front porch of the home and roses begin their bloom in April. Autumn hues from trees and the vineyards come forth late September through November.

Inside ceremonies are not allowed because of the historic preservation. Elopements and ceremonies up to a hundred are handled well in this location. The old resevoir once was in the back is spring-fed. This was a spring the Indians of the area came to often and has great historic significance.

PHOTO BY MATT KENNEALLY

LOCATION ACCOMMODATES

- Weddings Ceremonies - Elopements - After Hours Receptions
- Outdoor Only - Up to 200 guests
- Season: April through October
- A Preferred Wedding Services list is available.
- Music: non-amplified music
- Alcohol: check with park ranger
- Parking: limited
- Deposits: upon reservation of date
- Fees: information upon request

Phone: 707-938-9559 Park Guide, Michelle Kazerminejad
Internet
E mail:
Address: 3rd Street West, Sonoma, CA 95476

60 minutes from the Golden Gate Bridge. A map is needed for your guests. Your guests may stay at Sonoma Mission Inn, The Hidden Oak B&B, El Pueblo, Inn, Sonoma Hotel. Rehearsal dinners may be held at the Generals Daughter, Depot Hotel & Restaurant

- See the Day Trips section of this book for fun things to do while in this area.

GLORIA FERRER CHAMPAGNE CAVES
SONOMA ~ SONOMA COUNTY

PHOTO BY RAY BALTAR

The well known winery and champagne maker Gloria Ferrer is considered the "First Lady" of Sonoma. The beautiful vineyards are planted against the golden hills of California near the uppermost part of the San Francisco Bay. Amidst these vineyards sits the Mediterranean style building with red tiled roof which stands on top a knoll with the acres of vineyards spreading below.

Arched promenades extend around much of the building. The entry brings you into a lovely tasting room which is used to hold the reception and dancing. A flag-stone floor, beautiful long bar and dramatic fireplace bring warmth to the high ceiling. The terrace is beyond with a full view of the beautiful valley of vineyards. Flowers and blooming shrubs are part of the vineyard beauty.

This location speaks for itself. The building, vineyard beauty, staff, exceptional wedding

PHOTO BY MICHAEL LOEB

coordinator, and champagne are all top quality and have exceptional experience. This location knows how to bring a beautiful event to life.

An exceptional location.

LOCATION ACCOMMODATES

- Weddings and Receptions
- Indoor - 150 guests
- Season: Year round
- In-house consultant
- A Preferred Wedding Services list is available.
- Music: sound levels - monitored.
- Alcohol: Gloria Ferrer Champagne and wines
- Parking: ample
- Deposits: upon reserving the date
- Fees: upon request of packet
- Insurance: n/a

Phone: 707-773-0408
Internet
E mail:
Address: 23555 Highway 121, Sonoma, CA 95476

One hour from the Golden Gate Bridge. A map is needed for your guests. Your guests may stay in Sonoma at El Dorado Hotel, Sonoma Hotel, Trojan Horse Inn, Starwae Inn Rehearsal dinners Depot Hotel and Restaurant, The Generals Daughter, Magliulo's, Piatti or Zinos

- See the Day Trips section of this book for fun things to do while in the area.

HANNA WINERY
HEALDSBURG ~ SONOMA COUNTY

Hanna Winery sits atop a vineyard hill looking out over hundreds of prime Alexander Valley vineyard acres. The Mediterranean villa-styled Hospitality Center holds a romantic vantage point in the fold of the hills and western horizon. You can sip wine for two or hold an extraordinary wedding and reception at this location, the high beamed room and wrap-around deck bring your guests together in a memorable location.

The building is owned and designed by Dr. Elias S. Hanna, a noted cardiac surgeon. The winery expresses elegance in a peaceful oneness with the earthy setting. Hand carved Italian tiles accent the massive fireplace. High beams bring an echo of happy voices. Mahogany woods trim the arched windows and match a beautiful bar where wines are poured.

The facility offers excellent wines to guests. They are known for their Cabernet Sauvignon Blanc, Chardonnary, Merlot and Pinot Noir. 20,000 cases of wines are made annually from the 300 acres in several locations throughout Sonoma County.

A bridal dressing area is up the stairwell. The catering kitchen is new and well equipped for events large and small. Long summer evenings and remarkable sunsets are enjoyed from Hanna Winery. The colors of autumn are at their peak in this part of the valley by mid October and early November.

This is an exceptional winery experience

LOCATION ACCOMMODATES

- Weddings and Receptions, Indoor/Outdoor 100
- Indoor seating 100 guests
- Decks 75 guests
- Barrel Room 150 guests
- Season: year round events
- Time available: 4 pm to midnight
- A Preferred Wedding Services List is available.
- Music: Sound levels are monitored.
- Alcohol: Hanna Winery selections $7 corkage fee for champagne purchased independently.
- Kitchen: caterers kitchen
- Tables and chairs are included. • Deposit of 50% is required.
- Parking: ample • Insurance: proof required
- Deposits: required to reserve date • Fees: packet upon request

Phone: 707-431-4310 On-Site Event Coordinator
Fax: 707-431-4314
Internet:
Address: 9280 Highway 128, Healdsburg, CA 95448

A map is suggested for your guests. 90 minutes from the Golden Gate Bridge.

Your guests may stay at Camellia Inn B&B, Calderwood Inn, Madrona Manor or Geyserville Inn. Rehearsal dinners may be planned at the nearby Catelli's the Rex Restaurant & Bar, Giorgios Restaurant or Madrona Manor.

- See the Day Trips section of this book for fun things to do while in the area.

HANS FAHDEN VINEYARDS
CALISTOGA ~ SONOMA COUNTY

The famous painter Monet would have been very content capturing this lovely location on canvas. The mountain top views across thousands of timbered acres give a hint of the Swiss Alps and the vineyards of France. Pathways access the beautiful gardens which bloom around the pond. Roses grow profusely and spread up and over the frame of a charming roofed deck near the wine caves.

There are several ceremony locations. The decked area, as well as the small bridge which has a delicate arch, are ready for the photographer and a wedding couple's pose. There will soon be an enclosed room in front of the wine caves. Both caves and room will extend the ability to hold weddings and events inside and outside. Several words come to mind with this location: tranquility, reverie, romance and every adjective for natural beauty.

The family owned winery has spent many years developing the vineyards, property and grounds. To relax on the deck and look out over the exceptional view is a breathtaking venture. Their wine is highly applauded.

LOCATION ACCOMMODATES

• Weddings and Receptions
• Elopements, Rehearsal dinners
• Outdoor: - 50 to 100 guests maximum
• Wine Caves: guests maximum
• Season: outdoor - April through October
• Time: 5:pm to 10:pm
• Preferred Wedding Services list available.
• Kitchen: none, but power and water available
• Music: sound levels monitored
• Alcohol: Hans Fahden selections
• Tables and chairs: seating for 100
• Parking - ample
• Deposits: 50% of the fee to reserve date
• Fees: Upon request
• Insurance: required

Phone: 707-942-6760, Karen Fahden, by appointment
Fax: 707-942-4842
Internet Number
E mail
Address: call for appointment

90 minutes from Golden Gate Bridge on Hwy. 101 North to Hwy. 12 East. A map is needed for your guests.

Your guests may stay at Hilltop House B&B nearby, or in Calistoga at Mt. View Inn, Roman Spa, Wineway Inn, Dr. Wilkerson's Spa, Calistoga Inn, Indian Springs or the Pink Mansion and Silver Rose Inn. Rehearsal dinners may be held at All Seasons Cafe, Catahoula, Calistoga Inn Restaurant/ Brewery Gardens

• See the Day Trips Section of this book for fun things to do while in the area.

HOFFMAN HOUSE
GEYSERVILLE ~ SONOMA COUNTY

The wide platau stretching across the valley floor is abundantly planted with grapes. Geyserville, a tiny little town, is north of Healdsburg. The Christensens (father and son) have restored a fine turn of the century home. Leaving the stained glass, hardwood floors and charm of the period. The outside verandah is a pleasant place to sit.

The restoration of the fine old Hoffman house was just the beginning of the plans for this property. They designed and built the lovely Geyserville Inn with 38 guest rooms and pool next door and are developing a spacious vineyard area to hold lovely weddings.

The Hoffman House is comfortable for inside

ceremonies year round. The fireplace would be central focus point for a small indoor ceremony area.

By autumn 1997 the lawn area will include a shaded arbor, bbq, ceremony spot, and the complete beauty of the vineyards and distant mountains. You can even see the steam rising from the Geysers on the nearby ridge. Unlike the wineries, celebrations may begin at a variety of times throughout the day and be enjoyed early evening.

LOCATION ACCOMMODATES

- Weddings - Receptions
- Accomodations - Honeymoons
- Indoor - 50 guests - year round
- Outdoor - 100 guests - May - October
- Time: varies
- A Preferred Wedding Services list is available.
- Music: monitored for sound levels
- Alcohol: wine and beer
- Parking: ample
- Deposit: to reserve the site
- Fees:
- Insurance:

Phone: 707-857-4343 Location Manager, George Dutton
Fax:
Internet:
E mail:
Address: 21714 Geyserville Ave., Geyserville, CA 95441

90 minutes from the Golden Gate Bridge. A map is needed for your guests. Your guests may stay at the inn, Ye Olde Shelford House or Isis Oasis. Rehearsal dinners may be held on site, the Rex in Geyserville, or Madrona Manor

KUNDE ESTATE WINERY
KENWOOD, SONOMA COUNTY

The Kunde Estate Winery has extended an invitation to couples to be married and have their receptions within their premier vineyards. Located in the Valley of the Moon beneath the silhouette of the Mayacamas Mountain ridge is an exclusive and cherished setting. Most travelers find this to be one of the most beautiful spots in the world. The original 1882 stone winery walls of Dunfillan are part of this property. This is where the famous Hollywood star Geena Davis was married.

The historic Kunde barn was replaced by a replica building. It is now their tasting room and enjoys a setting with melodic fountains and ponds just outside the main doors. These massive doors open onto the decks and you view into the surrounding vineyards and oak trees. This gives an elegance not offered at many wedding locations. Ceremonies and receptions are a delight and well handled by staff.

There is intrigue and romance in having a wine cave event. This works well for smaller

PHOTO BY RAY BALTAR

— 106 —

ceremonies or rehearsal dinners. The tunnel into the hillside is thirty-two thousand feet and holds up to 6,000 American and French oak barrels.

In reviewing the site we were bounced across the hills of the family owned Kunde Ranch and Winery in a four-wheel drive. That was an experience in itself. It was a privilege to see portions of the 2,000 acre estate's 750 acres of vineyards. This vineyard was established over a hundred years ago from French grape stock. The Kunde family has owned it since 1904. In 1990 they released their award winning wines consisting of Chardonnay, Sauvignon Blanc, Cabernet Sauvignon, Merlot, Zinfandel and Port.

LOCATION ACCOMMODATES

- Weddings - Receptions - Rehearsal Dinners
- Tasting Room and Patio - 200 guests
- Estate Cave Dining Room - 40 guests
- Dunfillan Ruins - 300 guests
- Season: year round
- All wedding and receptions on Kunde Estate
- Winery must have a coordinator.
- A Preferred Wedding Services list is available.
- Music: amplified - monitored for sound levels
- Alcohol: Kunde Estate wines
- Parking: limited, valet for large groups
- Deposits: 50% required for date guarantee.
- Fees: Dunfillan $5,000 per day. Caves $2,000 per four-hour event. Tasting Room and Patio $5,000.
- Insurance: certificate of insurance required

Phone: 707-833-5501
Internet
E mail:
Address: 10155 Sonoma Highway 12, Kenwood, CA

A map is needed for your guests. One hour from the Golden Gate Bridge. Your guests may stay at Beltane Ranch, Gaige House, Relais du Soleil, or Flamingo Hotel in Santa Rosa. Rehearsal dinners may be held in the Kunde Caves, Kenwood Restaurant, Flamingo Hotel in Santa Rosa or The Generals Daughter in Sonoma.

- See the Day Trips section of this book for fun things to do while in this area.

LANDMARK VINEYARDS
KENWOOD ~ SONOMA COUNTY

PHOTO BY PAM GOSLIN

Without a doubt Landmark Winery and Vineyards is one of the most exceptionally dramatic vineyard locations Northern California offers. The California - Spanish style structure has a paver floored patio and courtyard with a lovely fountain. The backdrop and views over the well-kept vineyards include the beautiful Sugarloaf Mountain which stands as a silent sentinel. In the courtyard the wedding aisle is formed by terra cotta planters filled with flowers.

Several areas are available for your event. A small room with French doors leads onto a patio and lends itself to intimate weddings or rehearsal dinners. The tasting room has a colorful wall mural behind the granite bar. A variety of wines plus Mike and Mary Colhoun's award winning Chardonnays are available.

The location provides an on site Hospitality Staff to work out the details with you. This is excellent for handling a wedding from a distance. A nearby cottage is available in the vineyards for the families use that day. A bridal suite is included in the base fee. It is suggested you book a year or more in advance.

PHOTO BY MATT KENNEALLY

LOCATION ACCOMMODATES

- Weddings and Receptions
- Elopements are possible here.
- 150 guests maximum
- Season: Outdoor - April through early November
- Inside - year round - 130
- Dining Room -   50
- Tasting Room -   80
- Patio & Lawns - 150
- Time: 5:pm through 11:pm
- Preferred Wedding Services list available
- Selected catering
- Tables and chairs provided.
- Linens and table service provided.
- Music: sound levels monitored
- Alcohol: Landmark selections

Parking: ample
Deposits: 50% of the fee is required
Fees: Upon request
Insurance: not required

Phone: 707-833-0053 - Event Coordinator
Fax: 707-833-1164
Internet Number   http//www.weddinglinks.com
E mail
Address: 101 Adobe Canyon Rd., Kenwood, CA 95452

60 minutes from Golden Gate Bridge on Hwy 101 North to Hwy. 12 East A map is needed for your guests.

Your guests may stay at Relais du Soleil B&B, Gaige House B&B, Sonoma Hotel, or in Santa Rosa at the Flamingo Hotel or Creekside Best Western. Rehearsal dinners Depot Restaurant, Kenwood Restaurant Kunde Winery Caves (with caterer), or Flamingo Hotel.

- See the Day Trips Section of this book for fun things to do while in the area.

John and Carol Muir are the Innkeepers of a very romantic setting in the heart of Dry Creek Valley near Healdsburg. They bring talented, professionals together to create weddings, receptions, honeymoons, and other celebrations. All their diners and Inn guests feel welcome and well taken care of in this beautiful location.

This lovely eight acre estate surrounded by vineyards, but not within view. They are situated on eight acres of artfully landscaped gardens. The circa 1881 Victorian has nineteen rooms, a lovely honeymoon suite plus three other suites all with private baths. Eighteen rooms have fireplaces and some have balconies. The original Carriage House has nine rooms with a contemporary decor. The Garden Cottage offers complete privacy.

Many of the rooms are well appointed with antiques, Persian carpets and wall hangings depicting the period suitable

to the Inn. Victorian Theme Weddings are a specialty here. A pool is located near the Carriage House and citrus grove. Todd Muir is the Internationally acclaimed executive chef who oversees the excellent meals and wines provided the guests. They are noted in Gourmet Magazine, Country Inns and Travel and Leisure for their fine food.

The picture perfect wedding location can accommodate intimate weddings and receptions of 100 indoors, and when weather permits, the terrace brings your guest list to 155. A bridal dressing room is provided. Their wedding coordinator and staff will help you plan a perfect day.

Honeymooning here is ideal. Leisure afternoons at the pool, or fun things to do abound in the area. The coast is minutes away, and bike riding and ballooning are nearby.

PHOTO BY RAY BALTAR

LOCATION ACCOMMODATES

- Weddings and Receptions, Romantic Dinners
- Honeymoons, and Out of Town Guests
- Indoors - 100 guests
- In/Outdoors - 155 guests
- Season: Indoors - year round
- Outdoors - April through October
- Time: to be determined
- Wedding Coordinator - Vickie Latimer
- A Preferred Wedding Services list is available.
- Music: acoustical (non amplified) indoors - monitored
- Alcohol: all food and beverage provided by Madrona Manor
- Parking: room for 65 vehicles - shuttle may be required
- Deposits: 50% deposit to reserve date
- Fees: upon request
- Insurance: not required

Phone: 800-258-4003 or 707-433-4231 - Vickie Latimer
Internet: http://www.weddinglinks.com/
E mail: madronaman@aol.com
Address: 1001 Westside Road, Healdsburg, CA 95448

90 minutes from the Golden Gate Bridge. A map is needed for your guests. Your guests may stay at Madrona Manor, Honor Mansion, Camellia Inn or Calderwood. Rehearsal dinners at Madrona Manor, Southside Saloon, Giorgio's or Western Boot.

- See the Day Trips section of this book for fun things to do while in the area.

PARADISE RIDGE WINERY
A FINE WINE ESTATE
SANTA ROSA ~ SONOMA COUNTY

The most beautiful view in Sonoma County is claimed by this working vineyard and winery. No one would ever dispute their declaration. The California style, two story stucco building is found as you drive through oak trees and a surprise modern art display along the lane. The lane climbs the hillside (situated on 156 acres of well maintained vineyards) to

the hilltop where you feel as if you could see forever. And you can. From the expansive decks and terrace guests can enjoy breath-taking views of the Paradise

vineyards, the Russian River Valley and the coastal hills beyond. At night the valley's lights twinkle like diamonds on velvet. The terrace, with its sparkling fountains, offers a romantic area for

ceremonies and dancing under the stars. The Vineroom, with numerous glass doors opening onto the decks, provides a lovely dinner setting. A bridal dressing room is provided. Special rates are offered for Friday and Sunday weddings, and for the months of January, February and March.

The Bycks who own Paradise Ridge used to picnic on the hillsides with their children. They dreamed of their vineyard and an elegant winery to share with people who would want a special place to celebrate. Dreams do come true.

PHOTO BY MICHAEL LOEB

LOCATION ACCOMMODATES

- Weddings and Receptions
- Indoor - 150 guests
- Indoor/Outdoor - 250 guests
- Season: year round
- Preferred Caterer
- Preferred Wedding Services List available
- Music: sound monitored
- Parking: on site
- Alcohol - Paradise Ridge selections and keg beer
- Fees: Upon request
- Deposits: 50% to reserve date.

Phone: 707-528-9463, Marjke or Connie
Fax: 707-528-9481
Internet Number
E mail PARADISE@NETDEX.COM
Address: 4545 Thomas Lake Harris Dr., Santa Rosa, CA 95403

60 minutes from Golden Gate Bridge on Hwy. 101 A map is needed for your guests.

Guests may stay at Fountaingrove Inn, Hilton, Vintners Inn, Days Inn, Los Robles Lodge. Rehearsal dinners may be planned at John Ash, Equus, Los Robles, The Cantina, La Rose Hotel.

- See Day Trips section of book for fun things guests and honeymooners may do while in the area.

SOMMER VINEYARDS & ALEXANDER VALLEY FRUIT & TRADING CO.

HEALDSBURG, SONOMA COUNTY

On top of a vineyard covered hillside at the base of the Mayacamas Range sits a quaint Spanish California style building housing the winery for Alexander Valley Fruit & Trading Company. They have opened their doors for several years to concerts in the patio and lawn area. They now offer this pleasant, hospitable location to couples who want the romance of the vineyards as part of their wedding and reception celebration.

The facility includes bbq, grassy lawn and picnic tables with fruit tree orchards and vineyards everywhere. Caterers would bring most items on-site to provide food preparation. Power, water, plus a rustic serving bar is available for use. The flower edged patio has tables and chairs and a permanent dance floor for fun afternoons and evenings. This is one of the few locations which allow you on-site all day and throughout the evening.

Family-owned by Candance and Steve Sommer, the wine achievements are growing yearly in award-winning wines. This small family-run winery and food gift basket company sends their beautiful gift boxes all over the world. They honor the Alexandar Valley heritage of fruit orchards with their name. Dried fruits, mustard, jams and sauces may be found in the frontier style tasting room.

LOCATION ACCOMMODATES

• Weddings - Receptions
• Elopements - Rehearsal Dinners
• Outdoor only: 70 Guests
• Season: May - October
• Time: throughout day and evening
• A Preferred Wedding Services list is available.
• Music: amplified - monitored for sound levels
• Alcohol: Sommer Vineyard wines. Your selected champagne.
• Parking: ample
• Deposits: 50% to reserve date
• Fees: upon request
• Insurance:

Phone: 1-800-433-1944, Gary Sitton/Candace Sommer
Internet: AVFruit-trading.com
E mail: ssommer@sonic.net
Address: 5110 Highway 128, Geyserville, CA

2 hours from the Golden Gate Bridge. A map is needed for your guests. Your guests may stay at Honor Mansion or Calderwood Inn, Dry Creek Best Western in Healdsburg, or Hope Bosworth and Hope Merrill House B&B or Hoffman Inn in Geyserville. Rehearsal dinners Madrona Manor, The Rex, Southside Saloon, or Giorgio's Restaurants

• See the Day Trips section of this book for fun things to do while in this area.

SONOMA CATTLE COMPANY
NAPA VALLEY TRAIL RIDES
HORSEBACK WEDDINGS
SONOMA COUNTY ~ NAPA COUNTY

Lovers who love horses may wish to create a very unique wedding ceremony by horseback along the edge of the vineyards at Jack London Historical State Park in Sonoma County or Bothe-Napa Valley State Park which fringes the vineyards in the Napa County. This can be arranged by calling Sonoma Cattle Company.

The seasonal rides through Jack London's ranch will bring you to the Wolf House, through a redwood forest, out into May's Meadow and ride past Jack's Lake to the Bath House. There are several ceremony locations, and they even know an officiant who can ride and will marry you. The event may lend itself to period costumes of western attire.

Bothe-Napa Valley State Park in the Napa Valley area will trail you through lush redwood forests, along beautiful Richie Creek, and up into the very heart of the wine country. Vineyards, mountains, and dramatic terrain will be the setting for your photographs. We are certain our referral line will find you a riding wedding photographer to accompany you on the trail.

LOCATION ACCOMMODATES

• Season: April through November

Their service offers:
Professional Guides for
Full Moon Rides
Sunset Rides
Western Barbeque Parties
Group Rides

No children under 8 years of age
Maximum weight is 240 lbs.
Tennis shoes or boots
Phone: 707-996-8566
Fax: 707-9388366

• See the Day Trips section of this book for fun things to do while in the area.

TOPOLOS - RUSSIAN RIVER VINEYARDS
FORESTVILLE - SONOMA COUNTY

Topolos is a favorite dining experience for any occasion. Dining is indoors or outdoors under the latticed and vine covered patio of the historic 1879 farm house. Beautiful foods and fine service are part of the pleasures at Topolos. The public Greek-Mediterranean style restaurant is linked to the Russian River Vineyards unique Hops Barn-styled winery. Sheltered from winds, the outdoor dining is excellent for any event. They love doing rehearsal dinners, weddings and receptions.

Nestled into the hillside is the wooden structure of the winery which acts as the backdrop to a ceremony terrace. The cobblestone stone patio adds interest to the setting. There is a gazebo for the ceremony area also. The views here are of pasture, forest and vineyards.

SYLVIAS PHOTOGRAPHY

The adjacent Topolos Winery and tasting room is part of the working vineyard. Excellent wines that come from this winery are from grapes throughout the area. They crush, ferment, barrel, age and bottle Sauvigon Blanc, Fume Blanc, Pinot, Petite Sirah and several Chardonnays. Eighteen labels per year and seven are Zinfandels. Some of their producing vines are from 85 to 125 years old. These beautiful wines are available for your guests.

Bob Engel is chef and handles the restaurant with care and graciousness for each of the guests. The staff will work through various menus which specialize in a variety of Greek and American style dishes. The staff will help you design your day while on the property.

LOCATION ACCOMMODATES

- Weddings and Receptions
- Elopements
- Ceremony Area - 200 guests
- Restaurant - 100 guests
- Season: Year round for inside, Outdoor - April through October
- Time: Throughout the day/evening
- A Preferred Wedding Services list is available.
- Music: monitored - for sound levels
- Alcohol: Russian River Wines, plus beers and brandies
- Parking: ample
- Deposits: upon reservation of date
- Fees: Facility fee is $10 per guest
- Insurance: n/a

Phone: 707-887-1562
Internet
E mail:
Address: 5700 Gravenstein Hwy., Forestville, CA 95436

1 hour from the Golden Gate Bridge. A map is suggested for your guests. Your guests may stay at The Raford House Ferngrove Inn, Ridenhour Ranch House Inn, Santa Nella House, and Applewood an Estate Inn or at Holiday Select, Fountain Grove Inn in Santa Rosa. Rehearsal dinners may be held on site, at Chez Peyo, Equus Restaurant, Los Robles, or Farmhouse Inn

- See the Day Trips section of this book for fun things to do while in the area.

TRENTADUE
GEYSERVILLE ~ SONOMA COUNTY

The long, plum-tree lined road leads through acres of vineyards and curves into a grassy, shaded area with a latticed patio ready for special occasions. You have arrived at Trentadue, a working winery. The building was built in 1960, but some of their vines are a century old. Everywhere you look in this wide portion of the valley you will see grapes growing. Distant mountains wear white cloud bonnets, and the temperatures can climb. This lovely spot is an oasis of shade and vineyard enjoyment.

Vines weave throughout the lattice covering the patio. It gives a dappled effect to the shade. A small raised area of the covered patio is used for ceremonies or the music. Nearby lawns allow the party to expand with umbrella tables. Ceremonies may also be held on the lawn with the redwoods as a backdrop. Trentadue is now adding to this area a special event center room. This will enlarge the area to guests and expand the focus on comfort for seasonal weather and extend their events into the winter months. Gardens, lawns, redwoods, views of nearby hills, lovely sunsets, vineyards everywhere and

personalized attention by the on-site consultant will combine to bring your wedding dreams into reality. Couples especially enjoy the delightful twinkle lights and old fashioned street lights which provide a romantic summers eve glow. One has a sense of "old Italy" and the gardens of Tripoli.

The winery produces Zinfandel, Merlot, sparkling wine and a few desert wines such as port. They have an excellent gift area in their tasting room. Should you forget your toasting glasses, a selection is available here.

LOCATION ACCOMMODATES

- Weddings - Receptions
- Outdoor - 250 guests
- Seasonal: April through October. Use of new room will extend the season.
- Time Available: Five hour events. Choose between 8 a.m. to 11 p.m.
- Caterers from Preferred Wedding Services list available.
- Music: amplified is allowed - monitored.
- Party Rental Equipment: Site tables and chairs complimentary.
- Alcohol: Trentadue wine and champagne available at a 35% discount.
  Keg beer permitted - no hard liquor is allowed.
- Parking: ample
- Deposits: $500 non-refundable deposit
- Fees: 1-100 guests $2,000 and 101 to 250 guests $2,500
- Insurance: Required $500,000 liability policy.

Phone for Information & Booking event: 707-542-1235 ESP Event Coordination
Winery Phone: 707-433-3104
Fax: 707-433-5825
Internet
E Mail
Address: 19170 Geyserville Avenue, Geyserville, CA 95441

A map is needed for guests. Your Guests may stay at Ye Olde Shelford House, Hope Bosworth and Hope Merrill B&Bs and the new Hoffman House Inn or Honor Mansion in Healdsburg also Best Western in Healdsburg. Rehearsal Dinner may be at The Rex in Geyserville, Western Boot Steak House or Southside Salloon in Healdsburg.

- See the Day Trips section of this book for fun things to do while in the area.

VIANSA WINERY AND ITALIAN MARKETPLACE
SONOMA ~ SONOMA COUNTY

The red tiled roof and design of this winery is created from the Tuscan inspired charm of Italy. The courtyard entrance invites music and festivity for the location is private to you and your guests for the wedding and reception. Flower gardens, olive trees and views of the vineyards are afforded from this hilltop. Hand painted frescos enhance the walls of Viansa. The open, airy feeling along with the flagstone floors, barrel room and upstairs' marketplace grant you and your guests a "winery experience".

The family-run winery has a rich heritage of winemaking from Sam Sebastiani's background in wine blending. Viansa specializes in Italian Varietal wines. The many beautiful and bountiful recipes for receptions are created by Vicki Sebastiani. Food is prepared on-site with the freshest ingredients by the in-house kitchen staff. Four wedding dinner menues are available for your selection.

The Villa Courtyard and Hilltop Lawn are available for ceremonies, while Le Mura, an elegant garden building, with a white canopy offers dinner seating. A picturesque bridal dressing room is available by 4:00 pm for the wedding party to prepare.

The Tuscan meeting room becomes a bridal dressing room and is available at 4:pm for the wedding party to use. This room is adjacent to the cellar and provides access to all ceremony areas.

Vicki and Sam Sebastiani have placed their names together, "Viansa", and combined their beautiful wines and foods to give you the romantic experience your wedding day deserves.

LOCATION ACCOMMODATES

- Weddings and Receptions - 250 guests
- Minimum guests - 100
- Season: year round
- Indoor: 250 guests
- In/Outdoor: 250 guests
- Time: 6:pm to 11: pm
- Preferred Wedding Services list is available
- Alcohol: Viansa wine selection and beer available.
- Parking: available
- Deposits: A $500 deposit to reserve date.
- Fees: $1,000 fee for site use $4.00 per person additional for ceremony and reception

Phone: 707-935-4722, Event Coordinator- Dana Gracie
Fax: 707-935-7306
Internet Number
E mail
Address: 25200 Arnold Drive, (Hwy. 121), Sonoma, CA 95476

40 minutes from Golden Gate Bridge on Hwy 121. A map is needed for your guests.

Guests may stay in Sonoma at Swiss Hotel, Sonoma Hotel, Thistle Dew Inn, El Dorado Hotel or Sonoma Valley Inn. Rehearsal dinners may be planned at Viansa Winery, The General's Daughter, Piatti, Pasta Nostra, Depot Hotel and Garden or The Winemakers.

- See Day Trips section of book for fun things guests and honeymooners may do while in the area.

NOTES

HONEYMOONS

IN

VINEYARD

SETTINGS

BARTELS RANCH AND B&B COUNTRY INN
ST. HELENA ~ NAPA VALLEY

"One of the best places to stay in California" was bestowed upon the Bartels Ranch and Country Inn. No doubt, because every delightful detail into the romantic aspect of their client's desires has been met in this lovely location. Including bountiful breakfasts and bicycles.

Peaceful 10,000 acre vineyard and valley views from the windows and decks of this sixty acre estate lend complete rest and relaxation to the loving bride and groom. The Champagne Suite has a jacuzzi under the stars and a cozy fireplace for the cooler evenings. There are several other beautifully decorated and pleasure ridden rooms from which to choose with

private baths, robes, fresh flowers, candles and chocolates.

The massive gameroom holds several hours of repeated fun with fireside billiards and chess, the library offers books, periodicals and a piano. The nearby pond offers tranquility broken only by the bird's song. Old fashioned cookies, coffee and tea are served. An evening social with refreshments and dessert, are part of the daily fare.

Horseback riding, tennis courts and Chimney Rock Golf Course are nearby. There are nearby hills for hiking and endless antiques and galleries shopping trips. All this and wineries too.

LOCATION ACCOMMODATES

- Honeymoons - Elopements - Out of Town Guests
- Season - year round
- Summer/Autumn should be booked 6 to 12 months in advance.
- Mid week is often easier to book.
- Sixty minutes from the Golden Gate Bridge

Phone: Innkeeper, Jami Bartels 707-963-4001
Address: 1200 Conn Valley Road, St. Helena, CA 94574
Internet:
E-Mail:

Romantic Restaurants nearby: The Grill at Meadowood, Auberge du Soleil, Brava Terrace, Terra, Greystone, Pairs Parkside Cafe, Domaine Chandon, Showleys.

- See the Day Trips Section of this book for fun things to do while in this area.

FOOTHILL HOUSE
CALISTOGA ~ NAPA COUNTY

Situated within view of the vineyards and at the north end of the beautiful Napa Valley lies a very romantic bed and breakfast called Foothill House. The dreams, desires and details to a romantic setting are in this delightful environment. This is a country farmhouse at its best. Four lovely suites have been created for honeymooners or romantically inclined guests.

A separate cottage called Quails Roost is ~exceptional~. It sits on the hillside in back of the main house with views of Mt. St. Helena, vineyards and far off hills. The open airy feeling of this lovely cottage is enhanced by skylights, high ceilings, and windows. Quails Roost is a French pine accented suite with a four-poster bed. There is a window seat-reading nook, wood burning fireplace, kitchen, and a private patio. The bathroom has a Jacuzzi tub for two.

There are several lovely suites in the main house. A light and airy glass-enclosed dining area overlooks the yard and gazebo. This is where guests gather to enjoy the complimentary full breakfast, (breakfast may be served in your room). Special touches such as wine and cheese in the afternoon and fresh baked cookies are served.

The B & B is owned by Gus and Doris Beckert. Doris's desire to become creative with appetizers is set into action. When this occurs everyone is in for special treats. Doris is a trained chef and enjoys creating the bountiful breakfasts and exceptional food. They have been featured in several other publications.

LOCATION ACCOMMODATES

• Honeymoons - Out of Town Guests
• Season - year round
• In summer/autumn book 6-12 months in advance.
• Mid-week is often easier to book.

Hour & a half from the Golden Gate Bridge
Reservations: 800-942-6933 or 707-942-6933 Doris and Gus Beckert
Address: 3037 Foothill Blvd., Calistoga, CA 94515
Internet:
E-Mail:

Romantic Restaurants include nearby Showley's, All Seasons, Terra

• See the Day Trips Section of this book for fun things to do while in this area.

NOTES

NOTES

HILLVIEW COUNTRY INN
NAPA ~ NAPA COUNTY

Being surrounded by vineyards, fruit trees and herb and rose gardens are part of the pleasures experienced while staying in this lovely hundred year old home south of Yountville. The homey atmosphere for guests often begins in the kitchen early in the morning with coffee and a bountiful breakfast.

The rooms are comfortably decorated with walls stenciled to match the pattern in the decorator fabrics. Each guest room has a private bath, fresh fruit basket, queen size bed and windows with breath-taking views of the wide Napa Valley floor. The parlor includes a fireplace for you and other guests to enjoy. Evenings find you sipping wine and enjoying expertly created hors-d'oeuvres before you leave to experience one of the local "highly acclaimed restaurants" in the area.

Nearby the Wine Train moves slowly through the vineyards. The Comfortable farm house and gardens express Americana to visitors from around the world. Instead of wheat fields you view the vineyards.

LOCATION ACCOMMODATES

- Honeymoons - Out of town guests
- Season - year round -
- In summer/autumn, book 6-12 months in advance.
- Mid-week is often easier to reserve.
- 50 minutes from the Golden Gate Bridge

Innkeeper: Al and Susie Hasenpusch 707-224-5004
Address: 1205 Hillview Lane, Napa, CA

Romantic restaurants nearby include Piatti in Yountville, Compadres Bar & Grill, Cafe Kinyon or Bistro Don Giovanni. Domaine Chandon.

- See the Day Trips Section of this book for fun things to do while in this area.

THE INK HOUSE
ST. HELENA ~ NAPA COUNTY

It was like being aboard ship, climbing up the winding hardwood stairs into the beautiful day room atop the Ink House Bed and Breakfast. They call this the observatory and it is used by all of the guests for reading, art, relaxing and viewing the vineyards in all directions. Sunsets are spectacular from this enjoyable perch overlooking the valley and nearby Maycamus Mountains.

Built in 1884, in the Italianate Victorian style, this home offers seven beautifully styled guest rooms with five private bathrooms. Antique carved wooden and brass beds, delightful wallpapers, curtains and large oak furnishings lend to the feeling of "a step back in history". The huge backyard is meant for lounging or playing croquet. There is a beautiful barn toward the rear of the yard adding to the rural feeling.

Gourmet breakfasts are prepared with homemade breads, muffins and scones served with a warm hospitable spirit. Special wine pouring and appetizers and wine discussions are brought to the quaint parlor in the late afternoon or early evening for guests. You are in the heart of the wine country in this location. Bike riding, hot air balloons, the quaint town of St. Helena and vineyards are here to enjoy. Whether honeymooning, housing your wedding party, or out-of-town guests this is a lovely convenient location to explore the vineyards.

LOCATION ACCOMMODATES

• Honeymoons - Elopements - Out of Town Guests
• Season - year round
• Summer/Autumn should be booked 6-9 months in advance.
• Mid-week is often easier to book.
• Sixty minutes from the Golden Gate Bridge.

Innkeeper: Diane and David Horkheiner 707-963-3890
Address: 1575 St. Helena Hwy. (at Whitehall Lane) St. Helena, CA 94574
Internet: http://www.napavalley.com/inkhouse/
E-Mail: inkhousebb@aol.com

Romantic Restaurants nearby: Showleys, Pinot Blanc, Terra, and Green Valley Cafe & Trattoria, Tra Vigne.

• See the Day Trips Section of this book for fun things to do while in this area.

LA RESIDENCE' COUNTRY INN
NAPA ~ CALIFORNIA

Couples often say, "We want to go back again and again." That is what a honeymoon location should hold for each couple. Something so wonderful you want to savor it again and again.

La Residence holds you captive as you draw in the historic 18th century Revival styled buildings. The beautiful pool with gardens and an elaborate white gazebo are part of this well-kept location.

There are twenty rooms decorated and well appointed with antiques, beautiful four-poster beds, fireplaces, armories, superb bed and bath linens and French doors opening on to the patios, terraces and gardens.

Full breakfast are served to gusts in a lovely room with tables set for two.

You may be as private and discreet here as you desire. Wine and hors d'oeuvres are served at sunset.

The ~exceptional~ two-acre setting is shaded by hundred year old boundary oaks amidst acres of vineyards. The historic Mansion and the beautiful French barn called Cabernet Hall comprise one of the finest luxury inns the valley has to offer. Your hosts, David

Jackson and Craig Claussen have brought La Residence'from a B & B into the realm of a first class luxury inn.

LOCATION ACCOMMODATES

• Honeymoons - Out of Town Guests
• Elopements are handled elsewhere by their recommended consultant.
• Season - year round
• In summer/autumn book 6-12 months in advance.
• Mid-week is often easier to book.
• Fees average $175 - $215
• Fifty minutes from the Golden Gate Bridge

Phone: Reservations 707-253-0337
Fax: 707-253-0382
Address: 4066 St. Helena Highway, Napa, CA 94558
Rates: Upon request. Average $135-$235.
Internet:
E-Mail:

Romantic Restaurants include nearby Bistro Don Giovanni, Silverado Country Club, Domain Chandon and Piatte.

• See the Day Trips Section of this book for fun things to do while in this area.

NAPA VALLEY LODGE
YOUNTVILLE ~ NAPA

Napa Valley Lodge is adjacent to a vineyard in the quaint little town of Yountville. The spacious elegant lodge brings the California hacienda ambiance to guests with red tiled roof, patio and pool in an intimate setting. The decor is rich in color and textures.

A lovely breakfast is served with champagne at the poolside garden each morning. Creature comforts include the enjoyment of the whirlpool, sauna, spa and fitness center. The heated swimming pool and patio are included as part of your fun. The location offers magnificent views of the vineyards and nearby hills. Oak trees and colorful flower gardens add to the beauty.

The bedrooms are richly decorated. Deluxe amenities include a fireplace, private balcony or terrace, terry robes and the European-style duvet bed coverings.

This is a lovely setting in which to honeymoon or bring your out of town guests. They are a member of the Woodside Hotels & Resorts group, known for Monterey Plaza Hotel, Stanford Park Hotel, Bodega Bay Lodge, Lafayette Park Hotel and Half Moon Bay Lodge.

LOCATION ACCOMMODATES

• Honeymoons - Out of Town Guests
• Season - year round - honeymoons or wedding groups
• In Summer/Autumn season book 6-12 months in advance.
• Room Rates vary Rooms $152 to Suites $325
• 50 minutes from the Golden Gate Bridge

Reservations: 800-368-2468 or 707-944-2468
Fax: 707-944-9362
Address: 2230 Madison Street, Yountville, CA 94599
Internet: http://woodsidehotel.com
E-Mail: nvl@woodsidehotels.com

Romantic restaurants nearby include: Piatti in Yountville,
Vintners Court and the vineyard patio of Bistro Don Giovanni.

• See the Day Trips Section of this book for fun things to do while in this area.

OLIVER HOUSE
BED & BREAKFAST COUNTRY INN
ST. HELENA ~ NAPA COUNTY

A touch of Switzerland is in this lovely replica of a Swiss Mountain house. Tucked against the hillside along the Silverado Trail, the quaint inn reminds one of the Swiss chalets seen in the Alps. Clara and Richard Oliver's desire as innkeepers is to make you feel welcome and comfortable in one of their rooms, as in your own home.

Oliver House has a delightful 100 year old cottage which is my favorite. Resembling Hansel and Gretal's fairytale cottage, the fieldstone ivy-covered building has two levels. The woodburning stove and wicker settee are cozy below. One must climb a steep stairwell to a loft bed room, all part of the fun in this very pretty private spot.

The westward views are of vineyards.

Hundreds of acres spread out across the Napa valley. Two bedrooms are off the upper balcony in the main house and have French doors opening to a balcony. This is where lawn chairs and table are placed during the summer. A wonderful lazy spot to eat breakfast, read and sun, or sip wine and watch the sunset.

The bed and breakfast is well appointed with antiques fireplaces and private baths. Four-poster beds and feather beds are part of the enjoyment here. The big plus is the full breakfasts, complimented with home-made jellys and muffins are just the beginning of the full breakfast served.

LOCATION ACCOMMODATES

- Honeymoons
- Season - year round
- In summer/autumn book 6-12 months in advance
- Mid-week is often easier to book.
- Seventy minutes from the Golden Gate Bridge

Phone Reservations: 707-963-4089
Fax: 707-963-5566
Address: 2970 Silverado Trail North, St. Helena, CA 94574
Internet:
E-Mail

Romantic Restaurants include nearby Greystone, Terra, Auberge du Soleil and Trilogy.

- See the Day Trips Section of this book for fun things to do while in this area.

RUSTRIDGE WINERY
BED & BREAKFAST INN
ST. HELENA, CALIFORNIA

The true ambiance of a Southwestern Ranch style home with sweeping views of vineyards and oak trees await honeymooners and other guests in Chiles Valley. The completeness of this relaxing location is amazing. Honeymooners who want seclusion and a non-ornate but very attractive setting will find this ranch ideal. This is also an excellent place when out-of-town wedding guests have need for combined housing.

Contemporary bedrooms with featherbeds, fireplaces, decks for sunning are part of the romantic enjoyment. All rooms have private baths. A full breakfast is served between 9 am and 10 am. Tennis, hiking, bicycling sauna and water sports are just a few of the activities you may enjoy in this secluded valley.

An ideal bbq area with picnic tables would be a grand rehearsal dinner idea. A less formal setting, but fun. They will provide a preferred caterer's list to choose from.

This is a working vineyard producing Cabernet Sauvignon, Cabernet Zinfandel, Chardonnay and Riesling. Current wine releases may be purchased by guests for 20% discount.

They breed and race thoroughbred horses. The horses are exercised and trained on the ranch before they run at the track. They have several new foals each Spring.

LOCATION ACCOMMODATES

• Honeymoons - Out of Town Guests
• Catered rehearsal dinners - guests only.
• Season - year round
• In summer/autumn book 6-12 months in advance.
• Mid-week is often easier to book.

90 minutes from the Golden Gate Bridge
Phone Reservations: 800-788-0263
Fax: (707-965-9263)
Address: 2910 Lower Chiles Valley Rd., St. Helena, CA 94574

Internet:
E-Mail: rustridge@aol.com

Romantic Restaurants include Meadowood Grill, Greystone, Tra Vigne, Showleys or Pinot Blanc.

• See the Day Trips Section of this book for fun things to do while in this area.

SCARLETT'S COUNTRY INN
CALISTOGA ~ NAPA COUNTY

Just off the Silverado Trail along a brief vineyard surrounded lane is Scarlett's Country Inn. Set in a glen of oaks, pine and madrone, along with various fruit trees you will find a non-pretentious, homey setting. The tranquility and hospitality this bed and breakfast offers would bring anyone back into orbit. Scarlett loves housing out-of-town families prior to weddings and many honeymooners relax and enjoy themselves here as well.

The back deck area is beautiful with a pool and a grassy lawn for croquet or other lawn sports. This is not your usual resort -high- fly atmosphere with hundreds of activities going on. You create your own activities in the area from the multitude of adventures in this book or just take it easy.

The original farmhouse was built at the turn of the century. The country French decor and luxurious bedding of the Camellia Suite make this a special spot. Doors open onto a deck where star watching and sipping wine become a "must do" every evening.

The Gamay Suite has a sitting room which can house additional guests. There is a delightful old claw-foot bath tub in this room. Indian flints have been found along the creek in previous years. One of the bedrooms has been decorated in a masculine Southwestern motif. The Arrowhead Room opens onto a patio with a hammock.

Scarlett creates exceptional breakfasts for her guests and will serve them in their room, at pool side or at the dinning table. She has room for ten guests in her four rooms. This is one of the few B&Bs who will accept children as guests.

LOCATION ACCOMMODATES

- Honeymoons - Wedding Groups, Out of Town Guests
- Season - year round
- In summer/autumn book 6-12 months in advance.
- Mid-week is often easier to book.
- Sixty minutes from the Golden Gate Bridge

Reservations: 707-942-6669
Address: 3918 Silverado Trail North, Calistoga, CA 94515
Internet: http://mephers.aol.com/scarletts
E-Mail: Scarletts@aol.com

Romantic Restaurants nearby: Pacifico, All Seasons in Calistoga, Meadowood Grill, Greystone

- See the Day Trips Section of this book for fun things to do while in this area.

SILVER ROSE INN & SPA
CALISTOGA ~ NAPA COUNTY

This location receives ~exceptional~ for being the ultimate location for a romantic vineyards honeymoon. The Dumont family has designed the lovely Silver Rose Inn within this picture-perfect spot in the northern part of Napa Valley. There are two lovely sections to this location. Inn on the Knoll sits atop an oak-covered hill which floats above hundreds of acres of top quality vineyards. The newer portion of the inn, Inn In The Vineyard, sits amongst the vineyards with oak shaded decks, patio, gardens and swimming pool in your view.

All rooms have a theme to their decor. This brings a uniqueness to each romantic setting. Balconies, private decks, fireplaces, and enticing baths with Jacuzzi tubs bring couples into a very romantic backdrop. This is an excellent location to relax. The spa offers massage, hydro massage, herbal facials and water treatments, such as mud and seaweed baths. The entire inn is supplied by hot springs mineral water.

The gardens are planted with beautiful flowers, lawns, and trees. Each portion of the inn has a common meeting area where wine and cheese is served evenings and excellent breakfasts are enjoyed in the mornings. Bring your tennis rackets for the courts and your putter for the golf green. This is a sunny location, known for the warm summer evenings and bright starlit nights.

Guests may enjoy the Silver Rose Wine a recent vintage with their beautiful label. They have future plans for a lovely winery and restaurant on a different portion of 24 acre the property. No doubt it will be of the highest quality and standards as found in this location.

LOCATION ACCOMMODATES

- Honeymoons
- Season - year round
- Summer/Autumn should be booked 12 or more months in advance
- Mid-week may be easier to book.
- Ninety minutes from the Golden Gate Bridge

Phone Reservations: 800-995-9381 or 707-942-9581
Fax: 707-942-0841
Address: 351 Rosedale Rd., Calistoga, CA 94515
Internet: http://www.silverrose.com
E-Mail

Romantic Restaurants nearby: Calistoga Inn, Showleys, Tra Vigne and Meadowood, Trilogy, Napa Valley Wine Train

- See the Day Trips Section of this book for fun things to do while in this area.

SUTTER HOME INN
ST. HELENA ~ NAPA COUNTY

Pictures speak a thousand words when it comes to this lovely place to stay. It is situated in the center of Napa Valley. The carriage house of the fine Victorian home at the Sutter Winery has been made into lovely rooms for guests. They face onto a spectacular garden, intended for strolling and enjoying. The opposite view is of vineyards. Sutter Home winery creates award winning wines and the tasting room in adjacent to this location.

Each room has a private bath, queen size bed, fireplace. The continental breakfast is served in the beautiful main house. The

location is not as secluded and quiet as some of the honeymoon spots mentioned in this book, but certainly one of the most beautiful.

HOPE MERRILL & HOPE BOSWORTH
BED AND BREAKFAST
GEYSERVILLE ~ SONOMA COUNTY

A very special honeymoon location is in tiny Geyserville, a don't blink or you'll miss it town - in the midst of the vineyards north of Healdsburg. The two beautifully restored Victorians have received a first place award from the National Trust For Historic Preservation. This coveted award is

well placed. These homes are situated across the street from one another. They are beautifully furbished and landscaped.

The Hope Merrill has a small vineyard on the side near the relaxing swimming pool and covered side patio. The Eastlake Stick Victorian offers exquisite furnishings, a four poster bed, silk screen wall papers and lace curtains. The gracious hostess is Cosette and Ron Scheiber.

The Sterling Suite and Peacock Room are the more romantic of the lovely B & B accommodations. Each has a fireplace and sitting area. They have views of the vineyard and gazebo. Several rooms have spa or whirlpool tubs for two. There are twelve rooms to choose from between the two Victorians. Excellent breakfasts are served to guests in the lovely dinning area or patio at poolside.

These romantic Victorians are perfect examples of the Eastlake Street Victorian and the Queen Anne. Nearby are the Russian River and Lake Sonoma, great places to explore.

LOCATION ACCOMMODATES

- Weddings
- Honeymoons - Out of Town Guests
- Season - year round
- In summer/autumn book 6-12 months in advance.
- Mid-week often easier to reserve.

Phone Reservations: 800-825-4BED or 707-857-3356
Fax: 707-857-HOPE
Address: 21238 Geyserville Ave., Geyserville, CA 95441
Fees average $111 to $164. Two day reservation required on weekends
Internet:
E-Mail

1 hour from the Golden Gate Bridge. Romantic restaurants include Chateau Souveraign, Catelli's The Rex, Madrona Manor and the Southside Saloon.

- See the Day Trips Section of this book for fun things to do while in this area.

THE KENWOOD INN
KENWOOD ~ SONOMA COUNTY

Very few locations give the ambiance of a historical Tuscan villa as the Kenwood Inn and Spa evokes. The walled garden and pool area bring a relaxed atmosphere to any wedding or honeymoon. It is possible to do both here. Terry and Roseann Grimm, the proprietors, recently added several new overnight accommodations and an elegant spa to the original building and gardens. They all surround a lovely pool with delightful flower gardens. Fireplaces, private baths and a gourmet breakfast every morning are part of your stay.

Should you decide to inquire about holding your wedding here the Inn is exclusive to you and your guests. A very unique site for weddings and receptions for up to 125 guests. There are twelve elegantly furnished rooms for family or friends. This is an excellent location for retreat weddings. Though famous for their beautiful private weddings, they want to extend the invitation to honeymooners to enjoy the vineyard ambiance throughout the week.

The ivy covered Inn is nestled against a wooded hill and located off Hwy. 12 between the cities of Sonoma and Santa Rosa. The views are of the 1,000 acre Kunde Vineyards with the Maycaymus Mountains in view. Several state parks are nearby, as well as numerous wineries.

Pampering, privacy, and a glorious "European feeling" is graciously given to honeymooners in this intimate atmosphere. Down pillows, scrumptious breakfasts served poolside or privately, and a spa with massage and other services are part of the pleasures.

Staying in the artfully decorated honeymoon suite is part of the pleasure here, the pool, spa and bountiful breakfasts are to be enjoyed as you spend days exploring the wine country to your hearts content. The beauty of the Valley of the Moon will become a romantic memory. Nearby the town of Sonoma is fun to explore. A short drive will bring you into the Napa Valley, and an hours drive will have you listening to the crash of the waves on the blue Pacific shore.

PHOTO BY RAY BALTAR

LOCATION ACCOMMODATES

Honeymoons - Bridal Suite $350 per night Other rooms $265 per night Mid-week the rates are lower. Open year round. Rooms include antiques, lush fabrics, feather beds and comforters, balconies and terraces, plus private baths and fireplaces. Includes: breakfast and use of pool plus jacuzzi. Spa Includes: facials, scrubs, massage masks, wraps, stress reduction Inn Reservations: 800-353-6966

• Weddings and Receptions - 125 guests
• Season: from early May to November
• Time: throughout the day and evening
• Preferred Wedding Services List available.
• Alcohol - selections available through caterer
• Deposit & Fee Structure: Upon request

• On-Site Caterer: Pauli Halstead
• Parking - attendants provided.
• Chef Charles Holmes
• Music - monitored for neighbors

Phone: 707-833-1293 - Site Reservations, Caterer
Fax:707-833-1247
Internet Number
E mail
Address: 10400 Sonoma Hwy., Kenwood, CA 95452

45 minutes from Golden Gate Bridge on Hwy. 12 A map is needed for your guests. Guests may stay at the Victorian Garden Inn, Realis Du Soleil, Beltane Ranch, Trojan Horse Inn, Gaige House, or Sonoma Valley Inn-Best Western.

Rehearsal dinners may be planned in the Kunde wine caves with a caterer, Kenwood Restaurant, Generals Daughter or a casual patio dinner at Zinos Restaurant or Amadeos in Glen Ellen

• See the Day Trips section for fun things guests and honeymooners may do while in the area.

THE RAFORD HOUSE
RUSSIAN RIVER AREA ~ SONOMA COUNTY

The Raford House is where history and romance intertwine in the Russian River Valley. This lovely classic Victorian home was built in the 1880's by Raford W. Peterson and was part of the Wohler Ranch. It is a quality bed and breakfast run by Carole and Jack Vore who have combined their many talents to give their guests hospitality, great food, beautiful gardens, information and rooms to relax in.

The rooms are well appointed with antiques, canopied beds, unique wall hangings and mirrors. This is a perfect setting for a family wedding party preparing for the wedding day or a very special honeymoon in the Russian River area. The Strawberry Room looks out onto the garden and is especially secluded for honeymooners. Wine and appetizers are served to guests in the afternoon, as well as chocolates and a sherry nightcap in the evening.

Beautiful breakfasts are served in the large dining room or on the old-fashioned front porch. Either spot is comfortable and includes incredible views of the redwoods, vineyards and vegetable gardens across the valley.

Raford House is located near roads to the Healdsburg Dry Creek wine country, the Russian River playground and not far from Santa Rosa and those "city things" couples love to do. You can sit and relax, go to the river and canoe or take day trips in all directions.

Many couples love to return to the location where they honeymoon. This truly is a wonderful place to return to.

LOCATION ACCOMMODATES

- Honeymoons - Out of Town Guests
- Season - year round
- In summer/autumn book 6-12 months in advance.
- Mid-week is often easier to book.
- One hour from the Golden Gate Bridge

Reservations: Carole and Jack Vore 800-887-9503
Address: 10630 Wohler Road, Healdsburg, CA 95448
Internet: http://www.sonoma.com/lodging/raford

Romantic restaurants nearby include Chez Peyo in Sebastopol, Topolos in Forestville, Vintners Inn or Equus in Santa Rosa

- See the Day Trips Section of this book for fun things to do while in this area.

THE SHELFORD HOUSE
CLOVERDALE ~ SONOMA COUNTY

The Shelford House is Northern Alexander Valley's prize Bed and Breakfast. Everything from the porch swing to the exceptional antiques, period pieces and the collection of beautiful beds whispers by-gone days. The house sets perched above the vineyards.

The 1885 Victorian was built by Eurasthus M. Shelford. The ranch has grown fruit trees, hops and now viticulture abounds in the area. The handsome Queen Anne Victorian house offers three bedrooms. The two bedrooms upstairs each have a private bath The downstairs area offers a lovely room and bath. Three of the newer rooms are over the carriage house over-looking the vineyards.

A bountiful breakfast is prepared for guests and served at the huge dining room table. This stunning room has shelving and bookcases loaded with collections and books. Large windows look out onto the lawn and flower gardens.

Two unusual possibilities are offered here. A bicycle built for two to ride in the area, a couple ten-speeds or special wine tours are given in a 1929 Model A with a picnic lunch to follow. These are delightful ways to see the wine country.

The swimming pool is refreshing on a hot afternoon or after a long day of hiking and biking. The back deck offers a jacuzzi under the stars. Guest enjoy sipping wine and eating fruit and cheese in the lovely gazebo late afternoon. The setting sun is memorable from this perch looking west toward the Russian River.

LOCATION ACCOMMODATES

- Honeymoons - Elopements -Out of town guests
- Season - year round
- In summer/autumn book 6-12 months in advance.
- Mid-week is often easier to book.
- Ninety minutes from the Golden Gate Bridge

Phone Reservations: 800-833-6479 or 707-894-5956
Fax:707-864-8621
Address: 29955 River Road, Cloverdale, CA 95425
Internet: www.shelford.com
E-Mail: info@shelford.com
Romantic Restaurants include Chateau Souverain Winery, Bistro Ralph and Madrona Manor in Healdsburg.

- See the Day Trips Section of this book for fun things to do while in this area.

NOTES

HONEYMOONS

AND SOME

WEDDING

LOCATIONS

NEARBY THE

VINEYARDS

APPLEWOOD INN AND RESTAURANT
RUSSIAN RIVER ~ SONOMA COUNTY

This is an exceptional honeymoon location near the Korbel Winery, boutique wineries and vineyards in the Russian River area. While not in the vineyards, the appeal and luxury this lovely setting has needs to be written about for honeymooners. There are sixteen stylish guest rooms or suites. A very special honeymoon suite called the "Honeymoon Penthouse" is on a private roof-top deck. It offers views of the estates gardens and encircling mountains. A lovely fireplace with wicker chase lounge chairs are part of the scene. The romantically inclined will enjoy the spacious penthouse and a dreamy iron bed dressed with European down pillows and comforter. This is the ultimate for romance.

The pool and spa are just the beginning of unusual offerings in this lovely location. An excellent restaurant on site brings the location countless compliments from various magazines and books. The forests and gardens bring the perfect environment to a romantic retreat. "If Adam and Eve had take a honeymoon, they might have banished themselves to the new suites at the Applewood Inn" is a quote from Travel and Leisure, 1996.

LOCATION ACCOMMODATES

• Honeymoons - Elopements - Out of town guests
• Season - year round
• In summer/autumn book 12-18 weeks in advance.
• Mid-week is often easier to book.
• Ninty minutes from the Golden Gate Bridge.

Phone Reservations: 707-869-9093
Fax: 707-869-9170
Address:13555 Highway 116, Guerneville, CA 95446
Internet: http://applewoodinn.com
E-Mail stay@applewoodinn.com

Romantic Restaurants include nearby Cazanoma Lodge Topolos at Russian River Vineyards or Chez Peyo.

• See the Day Trips Section of this book for fun things to do while in this area.

THE BEAZLEY HOUSE
NAPA ~ NAPA COUNTY

The Beazley House has been a Napa landmark since 1902. Situated on a half acre, this lovely inn has become a romantic memory for many couples though the years. The family has created a warmth and friendly atmospher you will long remember and want to return to.

They are rated excellent with the AB&BA offering eleven suites within the Carriage House and Main House. Several are suitable for honeymoons, but I especially thought the Enchanted Rose Room was a delight. The king size bed and a whirlpool bath lead toward relaxation as does burning fireplace. Honeymooners are given complimentry champagne with Beazley House memento toasting flutes.

Weddings and special events are offered to small groups in the lush

gardens between the Carriage House and Main House. Sonja Beazley Burch will coordinate elopements or small retreat weddings up to ten guests. can host larger groups up to 75. They have several venues to offer upon request. Call Sonja Beazley Burch at 415-595-3670, she will coordinate your requests.

While the location is not in the vineyards, it is a romantic and private spot for honeymooners.

The access to San Francisco and the wine country from Napa allows for ease in exploring the area. The "town atmosphere" of Napa is a great example of American culture. Artists, music, fine chefs and history make the town a great place to explore.

LOCATION ACCOMMODATES

- Honeymoons - Elopements
- Retreat Weddings - 75 maximum guests
- Season - year round
- In summer/autumn book 6-12 weeks in advance.
- Mid-week often is easier to book.
- 60 minutes from the Golden Gate Bridge

Phone Reservations: 800-559-1649 707-257-1649
Address: 1910 First Street, Napa, CA 94559
Internet: http://www.napavalley.com/beazley/
E-Mail: jbeazley@napanet.net

Romantic Restaurants include nearby Vintners Court, La Boucane, Brix or The Wine Train.

- See the Day Trips Section of this book for fun things to do while in this area.

BLUE VIOLET MANSION
NAPA - NAPA COUNTY

Napa is known for their splendid Victorians. The recently restored Blue Violet Mansion is -exceptional-. Not located in the vineyards, but in the historic part of Napa. It has to be one of the most ornate and unusual Queen Anne Victorian locations in the U.S. They recently received "The best bed and breakfast in North America Gold award" by the Official Hotel Guide. The owners, Bob and Kathy Morris and daughter, Melanie Jones have restored and created a unique atmosphere by mixing excellent food, a warm friendly ambiance with romance in this majestic looking location.

Your first sight is the garden gazebo sitting upon a sprawling green lawn with flower beds. All three floors of this 1886 Queen Anne home are beautifully decorated. The rooms offer the ultimate of accommodations. The Morrises recently restored the third floor, calling it "The Camelot Floor".

These accommodations are designed with the theme of King Arthur and Lady Guenivere. Four romantic suites with hand painted walls and specific themes will step you back into England's history of kings and knights.

Some of the many services you may request are flowers, champagne, picnic baskets and romantic candlelight dinners for two and massage services in your room. The exceptional recipes served guests are as memory-making as the rooms. The Morrises are adding a new restaurant called Victoria - perfect for intimate receptions and rehearsal dinners. Elegant meals will be offered here with fine linens, crystal and silver. The glass conservatory walls will lend views of the pool and gardens.

LOCATION ACCOMMODATES

- Honeymoons - Elopements
- Rehearsal Dinners - Events
- 14 B&B - guest rooms from $145 to $285.
- 72 guests - garden events
- 49 guests - new Victoria Restaurant
- Season - year round
- In summer/autumn book 6-12 months in advance.
- Mid-week is often easier to book.
- In-house catering
- Parking: large groups may require valet parking
- 60 minutes from the Golden Gate Bridge

Phone Reservations: 707-253-Blue or 800-959-2583
Fax: 707-257-8205
Address: 443 Brown Street, Napa, CA 94559
Internet: www.bluevioletmansion.com
E-Mail: hkwx87a@prodigy.com
Deposit: 50%

Romantic Restaurants nearby include Chanterelle, La Boucane, and Bistro Don Giovanni.

- See the Day Trips Section of this book for fun things to do while in this area.

CEDAR GABLES
NAPA ~ NAPA COUNTY

A touch of old England is viewed in the design of Cedar Gables Inn, a mansion built in 1892 on the historic residential streets of Napa. Four fragrant cedar tree stand firm in the front yard shading the inn. Warm and rich tones are reflected throughout the rooms which are decorated with unusual antiques. Margaret and Craig Snasdell have spent many years developing the "special touches" for which this inn is known. They are a natural at hospitality and lovely food.

The comfortable parlor is a wonderful setting to bring guests together for wine and hors d'oeuvres each evening. The book shelves are filled with

books, and the room reflects rich warm colors, leather and unusual antique pieces.

Six rooms await couples. All with private baths, some with fireplaces and jaccuzzi. It is said honeymooners especially love the privacy of Lady

Margaret's room, a delightful room tucked away from the others. It has French Oak antiques, a private staircase, fireplace, and some unique wine barrel usage for decor. Many awards have been bestowed upon this fine inn.

The lovely mansion is set amongst several historic mansions in the city of Napa. Though not in a vineyard, this gracious location will be a happy memory. Consider the mansion for housing family and wedding guests for weddings in the area.

LOCATION ACCOMMODATES

- honeymoon - elopements
- out of town guests - bridal families
- In summer/autumn book 6-12 months in advance
- Mid-week is often easier to book, 2-day minimum
- One hour from the Golden Gate bridge.

Reservations: 800-309-7969, 707-224-7969
Address: 486 Coombs Street
Internet: cedargablesinn.com
E-Mail: mail@cedargablesinn.com

Romantic restaurants nearby include River City, Silverado Bar & Grill, Vintners Court, La Boucane

- See the Day Trips Section of this book for fun things to do while in the area.

MEADOWOOD NAPA VALLEY
ST. HELENA ~ NAPA COUNTY

Tucked into a wooded 250 acres on the east side of Napa Valley is the ~exceptional~ Meadowood. Though not in a vineyard, one must drive through vineyards to arrive in this stately country club atmosphere. The cape cod style buildings are located throughout the estate. There are seventeen gabled guest houses around the edge of the green meadow. A

lovely place to honeymoon, plan your ceremony and reception or have the families meet and get to know one another.

This is the location where it all happens. Elegant foods, romantic accommodations, a staff to bring full attention to your event and the 9 hole golf course, pool, croquet lawns and tennis courts. All this and the added feature of a well trained staff on the grounds.

Rooms feature fireplaces, private porches, down comforters, room service and luxury for wedding party members and honeymooners. The health spa offers strength and aerobic training, a variety of massage therapies, body treatments, steam room, sauna and whirlpool. You and your guests will find this an incredible location. Excellent focus area for retreat weddings.

A wedding brunch, buffet, or sit-down dinner may be planned with Meadowood's wedding coordinator. Vegetarian or savory meats and fish are prepared with flourish. They are known for their fine wedding cakes and deserts. Bon Appetit gave a rating as Best of the Year a "Weekend at a Resort," Country Inn's magazine awarded "Best In Dining" and Conde Nast Traveler readers listed Meadowood at number seven among United States resorts.

LOCATION ACCOMMODATES

- Weddings - Receptions
- Honeymoons - Elopements
- Indoor and Outdoor events
- Season: year round
- In-House Coordinator
- A Preferred Wedding Services list is available.
- Music: audio - monitored
- Alcohol: supplied and served by Meadowood
- Parking: ample
- Deposits: upon reservation of date
- Fees: events - upon request of packet, rooms - mid-week $295-435, weekends $355-525, suites -mid-week $500-1750, weekends $615-2175

Phone: 800-458-8080 and 707-963-3646
Fax: 707-963-3532
Internet:
E mail:

90 minutes from the Golden Gate Bridge. A map is needed for your guests. Your guests may stay at the Meadowood Resort. Rehearsal dinners may be held at Meadowood.

THE RIDENHOUR RANCH HOUSE INN
RUSSIAN RIVER AREA ~ SONOMA

On a tree covered hill above the nearby Russian River sits the lovely 1906 Ridenhour ranch house now owned by Fritz and Diane Rechberger. This bed and breakfast reflects the talents of this hospitable couple.

The warmth and charm of the interior of the home, suites and cottage reflect country English decor and American antiques. All set among lovely hillside garden paths of continuous blooms. Fritz brings his European award winning talents to the beautiful foods offered their guests. This is a very unique location which offers a four-course dinner. Fritz extends his talents for intimate gatherings, special luncheons,

and romantic wine tour baskets packed with unforgettable delights.

Six rooms and two cottages are offered. The Hawthorn Cottage has a fireplace and both Madrone Cottage and Hawthorn have queen size beds, and near the garden. A full breakfast is served guests. Fresh fruits, homemade marmalades, strudels, pies and creative egg dishes with local sausages.

Fritz is very talented in putting together beautiful feast for celebrations, inquire about their receptions or rehearsal dinners for their inn guests.

LOCATION ACCOMMODATES

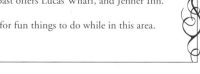

- Honeymoons - Receptions - Elopements
- Out of town guests - Rehearsal Dinners
- Season - year round
- In summer/autumn book 6-12 months in advance.
- Mid-week is often easier to book.
- 90 minutes from the Golden Gate Bridge

Phone Reservations: 707-887-1033
Address: 12850 River Rd., Guerneville, CA 95446
Internet:
E-Mail

Romantic Restaurants include nearby Cazanoma Lodge, The Farmhouse, Chez Peyo, and the Blue Heron. The Pacific coast offers Lucas Wharf, and Jenner Inn.

- See the Day Trips Section of this book for fun things to do while in this area.

SONOMA GOLF CLUB
SONOMA ~ SONOMA COUNTY

Elegant and within view of the vineyards is the historic Sonoma Golf Club. The tranquil setting of the golf course with a back-drop of the Mayacamas Mountain Range is picture perfect for a wedding. The red-tiled Spanish architecture brings the outdoors in. The vaulted ceilings and windows give an open and airy appearance to the rooms. This is a year round event location with several rooms, a lovely patio area and a garden area.

Near the circular drive entry the golf club has created a lovely garden and ceremony area with a modern gazebo. The backdrop of golf greens and hundred year oaks is breathtaking. Pathways lead by a lake which is a perfect location for photographs. There are 177 acres of visual beauty. Although the vineyards are at a distance across the greens,

PHOTO BY SYLVIA

your guests will be driving through the many acres of vineyards as they arrive for your wedding.

Their staff will customize your menu with your preferences or help you plan from many outlined menus. Table and glass ware and 4 hours use of Banquet facilities are included in meal pricing. A full bar, linens, professional cake cutting and a portable dance floor are part of the wedding package in this lovely setting. Their on-site consultant will help coordinate your event from a list of preferred professionals.

LOCATION ACCOMMODATES

- Weddings and Receptions
- Indoor and Outdoor Events
- Minimum - 50 guests: 150 for prime time Saturdays
- Indoors - 250 guests
- Outdoor - 500 guests
- Season: year round
- Time: throughout day and evening
- Alcohol: full bar
- Parking: ample
- Deposits: required to reserve date
- Fees: upon request
- Insurance:

Phone: 707-996-3483 Robin Chretien
Internet:
E mail:
Address: 17700 Arnold Drive, Sonoma, CA 95476

40 minutes from the Golden Gate Bridge. A map is needed for your guests.

Your guests may stay at the Gaige House B&B, Jack London Lodge or Sonoma Mission Inn. Rehearsal dinners may be held at Sonoma Mission Inn or Sonoma Valley Inn.

SONOMA MISSION INN & SPA
SONOMA ~ SONOMA COUNTY

Near the vineyards of historical Sonoma is a fine hotel called Sonoma Mission Inn & Spa. The 1927 hotel is designed to look like a California mission. The hotel is situated on eight acres of trees and lawns a few miles away from the vineyards in the Valley of the Moon.

As you enter on to the sleek tiled foyer you know this is the beginning of a wonderful experience. Whether you are there for a great meal at the Grille, to enjoy the spa and mineral waters, for your wedding and reception or begin your honeymoon, the Inn holds many venues.

198 rooms are available, making this a great place to bring a large group to enjoy a wedding with all the trimmings. The grandeur of the 20's is apparent at every turn. Aerobic studio, sauna and steam rooms plus two whirlpools and two a large hot mineral water pools are available to guests

along with tennis courts. A special
bridal package is offered to brides, it
includes manicure, pedicure, massage,
body scrub, facial and hair style plus
make-up application the day of the
wedding.

Whether on the front lawn under a large sparkling white tent with the
hotel as your backdrop or in the lovely Sonoma Valley Room, your
wedding and reception will be handled professionally by the well trained
staff and wedding coordinator of the Inn.

LOCATION ACCOMMODATES

- Weddings and Receptions
- Seated dining - 350 guests
- Sonoma Valley Room - 150 guests
- Sonoma Valley Room with food stations - 250 guests
- Sunday weddings are available
- Season: Indoors-year round
- Outdoor-April - October
- Time: varies
- In-House Coordinator required
- A Preferred Wedding Services list is available
- Music: audio - monitored for sound levels/time
- Alcohol: hotel catering and bar
- Parking: ample
- Deposits: to reserve date
- Fees: upon information request
- Insurance: not required

Phone: 707-938-9000 - Event Coordinator
Phone: 707-938-9000 - Hotel Caterer
Fax: 707-996-5358
Internet: www.sonomamissioninn.com
E mail: smiesmispa.com
Address: P.O. Box 1447, Sonoma, CA 95476-1447

60 minutes from the Golden Gate Bridge. A map is needed for your guests. Your
guests may stay at the Trojan Horse B&B, El Dorado Hotel. Rehearsal dinners may
be planned at the The Generals Daughter, Piatti, La Casa, The Kenwood Restaurant

- See the Day Trips section of this book for fun things to do while in the area.

THE PINK MANSION
CALISTOGA - NAPA COUNTY

This delightfully restored Victorian 1875 mansion is full of many surprises. The exquisitely furnished parlor and rooms, indoor swimming pool, back deck with gazebo and lovely bedrooms bring a full array of pleasures to the honeymooner or out of town guest.

Toppa and Leslie Epps now own the Pink Mansion. They are vigilant in taking care of the ornate structure and their guests. They offer six interesting rooms, some with fireplaces, all with views and/or decks to view the forest or town below.

The original owner William Fisher established the first stage line, carved out his vineyards and dug the wine caves for Schramsberg and Beringer Wineries. His home was known for social gatherings.

CALISTOGA MINERAL WATER METAL SCULPTURE

Toppa and Leslie will fill you in on all the great sites or encourage you to relax in their private pink mansion. They offer wedding consulting services and elopement arrangements are possible.

LOCATION ACCOMMODATES

- Honeymoons - Elopements - Out of town guests
- Season - year round
- In summer/autumn book 6-12 months in advance.
- Mid-week is often easier to book
- Fees vary between $95 and $195 per night
- Seventy minutes from the Golden Gate Bridge

Phone Reservations: 800-238-7465 or 707-942-0558
Address: 1415 Foothill Blvd, Calistoga, CA 94515
Internet: http://www.pinkmansion.com
E-Mail

Romantic Restaurants include nearby Calistoga Inn,

- See the Day Trips Section of this book for fun things to do while in this area.

THATCHER INN
HOPLAND ~ MENDOCINO COUNTY

The stately, three-story Victorian sits on the main street of Hopland. Built in 1890, the hotel housed stage coach and railroad travelers. The 108th anniversary continues to see it filled with happy guests throughout the year. The distant vineyards, fruit orchards and mountains provide the view. The railroad line nearby runs scheduled wine-tour trains through the area.

The twenty guest rooms have been restored with historic antiques and period elegance. The library with fireplace and comfortable chairs is the perfect place to sip wine and read. Everything from the hotel stairwell, huge mahogany bar and mirrors reflect a time gone by. Ron Hooper deserves the credit

for restoring this beauty. Carmen Gleason sees to the enjoyment of guests and runs the hotel along with her great staff.

Bedrooms are named after former Hopland pioneer families. Private baths (some tubs are claw-foot), brass beds, special wallpapers and drapery trims accentuate each room. The Thatcher Inn serves breakfast to its  guests in the front breakfast room and has a separate fine dining room with green Italian marble tables and period decor. A patio and deck for summer and autumn relaxation are just outside the door.

Thatcher Inn handles out of town guests, elopements and honeymooners. They often offer a mystery theater night and the casino, (Sho-Ka-Wah) is nearby.

LOCATION ACCOMMODATES

- Honeymoons - Out of Town Guests
- Season - year round
- In summer/autumn book 6-12 months in advance.
- Mid-week is often easier to book.
- Two hours from the Golden Gate Bridge

Phone: Reservations: 800-266-1891
Fax: 707-744-1219
Address: 13401 South Hwy. 101, Hopland, CA 95449

Romantic Restaurants nearby: Thatcher Inn,
Konocti Harbor Resort, Booneville Hotel

- See the Day Trips Section of this book for fun things to do while in this area.

VICHY SPRINGS RESORT
UKIAH - MENDOCINO COUNTY

The historic California State Park Vichy Springs has provided mineral waters to drink, bathe and swim for thousands of years. The beautiful setting is park-like with cottages and rooms which date back to the 1860's. Little Grizzly Creek ripples across rocks along-side several of the cottages making a wonderful sound as the water rushes past the 1880 Olympic size swimming pool on the property.

The 20 rooms are nicely decorated with matching coverlets and window decor. Individual baths and privacy for relaxation are part of this hideaway. Walking the trails on the 700 acres is an invitation to meet nature of all types. The spa offers Swedish therapeutic massage, herbal facials and individual baths in the hot mineral water. This would be a quiet retreat after a whirlwind wedding.

Poolside there is a lovely, carpeted room with a full kitchen in which a caterer may create a rehearsal dinner for family and friends if you are being married in the area.

LOCATION ACCOMMODATES

• Honeymoons - Out of Town Guests - Rehearsal Dinners
• Season - year round
• In summer/autumn book 6-12 months in advance.

Two hours from the Golden Gate Bridge

Phone: 707-462-9515, Gilbert and Marjorie Ashoff
E-Mail: vichy@pacific.net
Address: 2605 Vichy Springs Road, Ukiah, CA 95482
Fax: 707-462-9516

Romantic Restaurants nearby includes Thatcher Inn.

• See the Day Trips Section of this book for fun things to do while in this area.

NOTES

*The preceding pages give a good feel
for the different season in the
vineyards not all photos
are wedding sites.*

WINTER

SPRING

PHOTO BY CREATIVE FOCUS

SUMMER

PHOTO BY BARTELS

PHOTO BY JOSHUA B. ROTSTEN

Autumn

DAY TRIPS IN THE
WINE COUNTRY

The day trips allow you to travel throughout the entire region with the knowledge that each of the locations and restaurants have something great to offer you. Phone numbers make it convenient for you to set your reservations from afar or while in the area.

It is recommended because of the popularity of many of the businesses mentioned that you set your appointments well in advance of your being in the area.

Table of Contents   County

Day Trips Index To Extended Information For The Areas

WeddingLinks Northern California — http//www.weddinglinks.com/

Wedding and Honeymoon Location information for Northern California

Coastal from Marin to Mendocino

Bodega Bay Chamber of Commerce 707-875-3422

Ft.Bragg Coast Chamber 800-726-2780

         www.mendocinocoast.com

Marin Coast Visitors Bureau 415-472-7470

Mendocino County Convention and Visitors Bureau 707-961-6300

DAY TRIPS IN THE
WINE COUNTRY

The following informative pages have been created for couples who come to the vineyards of Northern California for a variety of reasons surrounding romance, marriage and honeymoons.

For the many couples who invite hundreds to a vineyard wedding it has become increasingly popular to create an Itinerary For Your Guests While In The Area. This often includes, things which may be done together as a group, leading up to the wedding, or experience the days following the event. The book achieves this for you. It suggests some of the places and things to see while in the area(s) and makes the phone numbers available for information or scheduling reservations.

For the couple who plan to bring a few friends or family to their vineyard ceremony the book gives selections of sightseeing, restaurants and lodging for all to enjoy while in the area. If wine tasting is the goal, it designates some of the "not to miss" wineries. Decide together some of the fun things you would like to do while in the area and check them off in the book.

For couples eloping and/or honeymooning in the wine country these day trips are complete to each of the wine regions in Northern California allowing you to plan a perfect, romantic and enjoyable time while here. Look in the "Honeymoon Section" of this book to learn about the honeymoon vineyard locations. Look in the box portions of the pages on Vineyard Wedding and Reception Locations to see if they will offer an elopement service at that wedding site.

DAY TRIPS IN THE
WINE COUNTRY

Publications and Services specific to these areas. Inquiring about these ahead of time will inmprove the enjoyment of your trip to the vineyards.

Radio Station for Sonoma County's up-to date events Q105

or call 707-270-5105

Sonoma Traveler Magazine ....www.winetravel.com

Sonoma Valley Guide Magazine 1-800-651-8953

Sonoma Wine Country Inns 800-295-9463

V.I.T. Very Important Taster 2 for 1 Card available for tasting in wineries for Sonoma and Napa 707-963-9597

Wine Country Referrals for B&B 707-942-2186

San Francisco

S.F. Visitors Bureau ....http://www.travelfile.com

Whats Happening (in-town events) 415-391-2001

Up-to date events internet ....http://www.sfgate.com

B&B International Reservations 415-696-1690

Hotels and Lodging in S.F. 800-374-7787

California Discount Hotel Rates 415-252-1107

Alegro Private Tours ....415-668-1864.

Vets Taxi 415-552-3181

DAY TRIPS IN THE
WINE COUNTRY

Day Trips Index To Extended Information Continued
Lake and Mendocino - Inland

Napa Area

Sonoma County

NAPA COUNTY

#1

DAY TRIP

TO

ST. HELENA

AND

CALISTOGA

GREAT PLACES TO STAY

Scarlett's Country Inn is located in the vineyards along the Silverado Trail. Homey, friendly, with wooded gardens and pool Four suites are available, 707-942-6669.

Meadowood Resort is nearby on the Silverado Trail. This beautiful New England styled resort surrounds a beautiful golf course with cottages, croquet courses, pool and offers an excellent restaurant, 800-458-8080.

Villa St. Helena sits atop the Macaymas Mountain range above St. Helena. Created in 1941 as a retreat for the stars and politicians, it is said to have quite a history, 707-963-2514.

In Calistoga along the Silverado Trail the beautiful Silver Rose Inn sits atop a wooded knoll and looks out over vineyards. The spa, massage, pool and lovely rooms make this an enjoyable and romantic stay, 707-942-9581.

Larkmead Country Inn located near Calistoga is a two story B&B in a vineyard setting. 4 Lovely rooms appointed with antiques and history. A continental breakfast is served, 707-942-5360.

Wine Way Inn is located in Calistoga. A cozy B&B with a wonderful back deck and delightful rooms. The treasure of letters added to by the guests throughout the years are waiting to be read in the night stand drawers of each room. George the dog brings his talents to each visitor, 800-572-0679.

The Elms is a romantic Victorian in Calistoga. Next door to a lovely city park with gazebo. It is truly a setting for romance. Furnished with European antiques and warm hospitality. A special honeymoon cottage is available, 800-235-4316 or 707-942-9476.

Outdoor Fun

St. Helena Cyclery has your rental needs for great bike touring. Call ahead for information, 707-963-7736.

V. Sattui Winery in St. Helena has a wonderful deli and picnic area under the oaks. Or take your picnic lunch to Stonesbridge Park which is located on Pope Street and is perfect for a picnic spot along the Napa River. The historic Bale Mill offers a lovely picnic spot, as do many of the wineries along the way. 707-963-7774

The Calistoga Gliderport will take you up and over the beautiful vineyards gliding you to the earth in an exciting adventure aloft. Weather permitting - which it usually does, 707-942-5000.

Antique Tours Limousine Service lend a festive air in 1947 Packard Convertibles, 707-226-9227.

Bonaventura Balloon Company floats you over the picturesque vineyards serving brunch, proposals, weddings, small group excursions. Breathtaking colorful experiences, 707-944-2822.

Napa Valley Balloons include a breakfast at Domaine Chandon, 800-564-9399 or 707-253-2224.

Get Away Bike Vacations in Calistoga can plan all types of adventures for two, to two-hundred, 707-942-0332.

FUN THINGS TO DO

In St. Helena tour the Culinary Institute of America and enjoy the cookbook and culinary equipment store. While there, eat at the exciting Greystone Restaurant staffed by Culinary Institute grads. The building was formerly Christian Brothers Winery built in 1889. Reservations 707-967-1100.

In St. Helena the Las Cerezas/Napa Wine Label Company will design you a personal wine label and apply it to cases of their fine wine, 707-963-9597. Great wedding favors and gifts for attendents.

The Silverado Museum houses thousands of items from Robert Louis Stevenson's history and memorabilia. He loved the area and honeymooned on the side of Mt. St. Helena, 707-963-3757.

Vintage Hall/Napa Valley Museum is located in the old St. Helena High School building. A great way to learn about the valley, people and the wines. A special area is devoted to the Wappo Indians who lived in the valley for centuries, 707-963-7411.

Spas such as Lavendar Hill at 707-942-4495, Eurospa at 707-942-6829, Golden Haven at 707-942-679, and Nance's Hot Springs at 800-201-6211 or 707-942-6211, are some of the fine hot water spas in the area.

The Sharpsteen Museum is a must see. It outlines the beginnings of Calistoga. The art and creative diorama design was completed by one of the first Walt Disney artists, Ben Sharpsteen, 707-942-5911.

Calistoga Mineral Water located on the Silverado Trail has an excellent tour to offer, 707-942-6295.

WINE TASTING

Sequoia Grove Winery has a beautiful stand of redwoods and a 1860 barn just south of St. Helena. The wine will please your pallet with fine Cabernet Sauvignon. The Estate Reserve Chardonnay and Carneros Chardonnay are a few of the "must taste wines". Located on Hwy 29, 707-944-2945.

Newton vineyards is set on a hill overlooking the valley. A unique roof garden of roses makes this a delightful perch to view the valley floor. Their wines of Merlot, Cardonnay are oak aged and housed underground, 707-963-9000 by appointment.

Sutter Home Winery and the Zinfandel Gardens are a must see at any season. Eight hundred varieties of flora with the backdrop of a Victorian home. The Zinfandels, Chardonnay and Cabernet are but a few of the wines produced Trinchero family has made famous, 707-963-3104.

You won't want to miss the cave and winery tour at Beringer Winery. The 1876 Rhine House is a German style Victorian. The caves were dug into the hillside by Chinese labor. Their Chardonnay and Cabernet are famous in the wine world, 707-963-7115.

Sterling, near Calistoga provides a delightful trip on the gondola to the top of the hill into a white walled winery. The beautiful terraces and patios lend an ambiance to the excellent Merlot, Chardonnay and Cabernets, 707-942-3344.

French methode champenoise, a sparkling wine, may be enjoyed at Larkmead-Kornell Cellars. Make certain to stop at Cuvaison, Winery, Clos Pegas, and Hans Fahden Wineries are amongst the many.

SHOPPING MANIA

Hurd Candles just North of St. Helena offer beautiful designs in candles and wax creations. Located in a historic stone building along with two restaurants, Freemark Abbey Wine and a great gift store. Its a fun shopping stop, 707-963-9211.

Main Street of St. Helena is fun to explore. Vanderbilt and Company has some of the finest selections and collections in the valley. Local artist's works may be found at The Gallery on Main Street Estate jewelry, 707-963-1010.

The town of Calistoga looks like something out of the old west. Some fine art studios are located here, as well as, Evans Ceramics Gallery. A great town for strolling at anytime of day or evening.

The All Season Wine Shop in Calistoga is the "Knowledge Shop" for the small specialty wineries in the area. They can help you create a case of selected fine wines, 707-942-6828.

GREAT PLACES TO EAT FROM
ST. HELENA TO CALISTOGA

Coffee - expresso plus lovely baked items and fresh juice may be found at Napa Valley Coffee Roasting Co. in St. Helena, 963-4491.

Model Bakery is the best bread in Napa Valley - espresso too.

Breakfast at the Grill at Meadowood near St.Helena will quiet the grumblies of any hungry morning person, 707-963-3646.

Lunch and dinner may be enjoyed at Pairs Parkside Cafe. Colorful and a varied menu of beautifully presented foods, 707-963-7566.

Breakfast & Lunch at Magnolia Cafe in St. Helena, 707-963-0748.

Terra, tho a little more posh, is an excellent choice for dinner. Their excellent food and wine is widely known, 707-963-8931.

Lunch or dinner at Greystone in St. Helena, 707-967-1010 Dinner on the deck at Brava Terrace is a touch of Provence and Italy, California and Mediterranean faire, 707-963-9300.

Pacifico in Calistoga offers all three meals, 707-942-4400. Dining on the patio at Calistoga Inn is delightful, especially on a warm summers eve. You can enjoy the Brewery Lagars. Sunday Brunch available, 707-942-4101.

All Seasons Cafe in Calistoga offers excellent lunch and dinners. One of the best and affordable of wine lists in the area, 707-942-9111

COASTAL

$^{\#}2$

DAY TRIP
THROUGH
MARIN
SONOMA
AND
MENDOCINO
COUNTIES

GREAT PLACES TO STAY

Marin Coast

Stinson Beach offers Casa Del Mar, a Mediterranean villa with hillside gardens looking out over the Pacific ocean. Beach is 2 blocks from the inn. Memorable breakfasts, 415-868-2124.

In Olema, the Olema Inn is a Victorian with excellent food and beautifully furnished rooms, 415-663-9559. A lovely garden and patio area has been created for weddings and events.

Pt. Reyes Seashore Lodge is a beautiful re-creation of a turn of the century lodge with woods, views, lawns, excellent furnishings On Hwy. 1 in Pt. Reyes, 415-663-9000.

In Inverness, Manka's Lodge and Restaurant is rustic and enjoyable tucked up against the hillside. 415-669-1034.

Tom Evans, of Pt. Reyes Country Inn has a cottage on Tomales Bay plus a lovely B&B in Pt. Reyes, 415-663-9696.

Dancing Coyote Beach overlooks the Tomales Bay with a tiny beach. These cottages have fireplaces and decks over the water. Kitchens are also available, 415-669-7200.

Blackthorne Inn is in a wooded canyon, this romantic B&B gives the feeling of being on top of the world. Full breakfast, 415-663-8621.

OCEAN TIPS

Whale Watching is best between December and the end of February.

Swimming is hazardous along most of this coast, rip tides and sneaker waves that pull you out are common. Neither wind surfing nor swimming is recommended on Tomalas Bay because of the white sharks in the bay waters.

Scuba diving is popular at Stillwater Cove County Park, Salt Point State Park and continues North at the many coves and beaches. Wet suits are advised, the surf, temperature and currents are extreme.

GREAT PLACES TO STAY

Sonoma Coast

Bay Hill Mansion is a neo Queen Anne Victorian on a hill overlooking the Bodega Harbor. View and great full breakfast, deck, hot tub, Hors d'oeuvres and wine in the evenings, 707-875-3577.

Bodega Bay and Beyond has a selection of lovely beach homes to rent for a weekend, week or month, 800-888-3565 or 707-875-3942 http://www.sonomacoast.com and E-Mail reservations@ap.net

Bodega Bay Lodge has ocean views from their Bodega Harbor setting high on a bluff overlooking the bay. Restaurant, hot tub, decks and a peaceful atmosphere, 707-875-3525.

Sonoma Coast Villa is inland toward the picturesque town of Bodega. This exceptional Mediterranean Villa has six elegant rooms with fireplaces, pool and lovely verandas. http:www.scvlla.com Call 888-404-2255 or 707-876-9818.

Jenner Inn has cottages with dramatic ocean views, and forty other guest rooms in a variety of accommodations, 707-865-2377.

The Sea Ranch Lodge is above Jenner on Hwy 1 and offers a 20 room Inn with views of the ocean. Tennis, swimming pool and sauna are available along with private beach trails. 800-SEA-RANCH Vacation Home Rentals, 707-785-2579.

Coast Guard House in Point Arena is a Cape-Cod style home overlooking a lighthouse and the ocean. Six rooms are available with continental breakfast, 707-882-2442.

GREAT PLACES TO STAY

Timber Cove Inn has ocean views, 47 rooms with baths are available, many have hot tubs and fireplaces. Cozy and complete with a fine restaurant which offer food with a French flair, 707-847-3231.

Mendocino Coast

Breakers Inn is a new luxury Inn offering 27 rooms and some suites with kitchens. Beautiful ocean views in Gualala, 800-BREAKER.

The Gualala Hotel is a 1903 historic two-story hotel. Formerly a stage-coach stop, it sports 19 rooms and baths are shared as in days of the early West. Five rooms have private baths. 707-884-3441

St. Orres is a unique inn on the coast near Gualala. Cottages, rooms have ocean views, decks and a quality restaurant. Stained glass windows and ornate towers give a Russian architecture emphasis, 707-884-3303.

The MacCallum House is a exceptional 1882 Victorian B&B. The House, Carriage House and Barn all house antiques and are set on park-like lawns with ocean and garden views. Rich woods, fieldstone fireplace in the lovely restaurant is a very romantic setting for lovers, 707-937-0289 or 1-800-609-0492.

Little River Inn must be reserved well in advance. The white farmhouse is a replica of New England. 66 units have private baths and vary from cozy cottages to small houses. Most have views and fireplaces. Jacuzzis and T.V. are available, 707-937-5942.

Elk Cove Inn offers an elegant escape to oceanfront cottages. Gazebo, gardens, beach, and oceanfront dining room, 800-275-2967.

GREAT PLACES TO STAY

Seclusion and romance are alive at Agate Cove Inn B&B. It overlooks the coast in Mendocino. Several cottages with fireplaces are landscaped with flower gardens on the hillside. Several rooms have four-poster beds. Seaviews and excellent full breakfast are served along with memorable sunsets, 707-937-0551. e-mail agate-cove@juno.com

Historic gardens, nestled between the coastal forests and the ocean are the home of the Stanford Inn by the Sea. Beautiful wood decor with fireplaces, lush beds, pool sauna and spa, plus exceptional views of Mendocino bay are part of the many pleasures here, 1-800-331-884 or 707-937-5615. e-mail stanford@stanfordinn.com

Fort Bragg provides "excellence" with the Gray Whale Inn. There is romance in every corner of this historic redwood inn. Private baths, views of the ocean or town, and cozy comforts, 1-800-382-7244 or 707-964-0640.

FUN THINGS TO DO

Stinson, Pt. Reyes, and Sonoma Coast are full of exceptional art galleries. Potters, artists, jewelsmiths and studios abound.

Exploring the Victorian town of Mendocino will take days. The T.V. series "Murder She Wrote" has been filmed here for years. There are a multitude of shops of every art, craft, book, and art classes are taught at various times. Truly an art colony.

Ft. Bragg offers the Guest House Museum featuring the history of their logging industry.

The Skunk Train moves through the redwood forest from Ft.Bragg to Willits, half-day trips are available on this narrow gauge railroad. It helps to have reservations ahead, 707-964-6371.

OUTDOOR FUN

Hiking trails at Pt. Reyes Lighthouse and throughout the National Park - bring a jacket, its usually windy and cool. Bear Valley Visitors Center offers maps, trail guides, and schedules of the nature programs, 415-663-1092.

State Park Taylor Redwoods offers hiking trails, picnic areas and bbq for day use areas, 415-488-9897.

Ocean fishing is offered at Lawsons Landing in Dillon Beach, 707-878-2443 and at Bodega Bay's Spud Pt. Marina on Jaws, 707-875-3495. Crab, cod and salmon fishing are known here.

Golf courses are the Bodega Harbor golf Links, 707-875-3538 Sea Ranch Golf Links offers a 9 hole course, 707-785-2467 Little River Golf & Tennis Club has a 9 hole course, 707-937-5667.

Fort Ross is a restored Russian Fort along the coast. An excellent opportunity to learn how the coast was first settled by fur traders from Russia in 1812. A great book store in this Visitor's Center.

Van Damm St. Park is a varied and spectacular park. Camping, hiking and a small beach await the visitor, 800-444-7275.

Catch a Canoe and Bicycle Too offers all types of rentals. for your outdoor pleasures, 707-937-0273. www.destinate.com

Mendocino Coast Botanical Gardens is a "must see." 47 acres on a bluff near Ft.Bragg are the showcase of rhododendrons between April and June. Trails move between roses, camellias, fuchsias, and hundreds of native plants, 707-964-4352.

STORE MANIA

Stinson Beach and Pt. Reyes Station offer a variety of art and crafts along the way. Many local artists sell works in these stores. Don't forget the wonderful salt water taffy along the way.

Candy & Kites/Harbor Kites have an unusual variety of kites to fly. Colorful and fun to soar at the local beaches. Located in Bodega Bay.

The Wren Gallery in Bodega Bay brings exciting art from a variety of artists.

The entire town of Mendocino is one delightful store after another.

Mendocino Farmers Market on Fridays from May - October 2 p.m. on.

GREAT PLACES TO EAT

Huge breakfasts are served at the Station House Cafe in Pt. Reyes. Their lunch and dinner menus are varied and they have a nice garden to enjoy, 415-663-1515.

Gualala Hotel Restaurant offers bountiful breakfasts and hearty lunches and dinners. Prime Rib on Saturday evening 707-884-3441.

Mendocino Bakery & Cafe offer espresso or cappuccino with pastry. Later in the day lunches and dinners are created. 707-937-0836.

Cafe Beaujolais is the "find of the year" for breakfast, lunch, dinner, or desert. Call for reservations at the lovely Victorian house and garden. Mendocino Chef and writer Margaret Fox has written two cook books, 707-937-5614.

Bay View Cafe offers fantastic breakfasts, filling lunches and a pasta and steak menu for dinner. 707-937-4197.

Picnics baskets are replenished at:
  Olema Hotel Deli in Olema
  The Food Company in Gualala, 707-884-1800.
  Good Taste in the town of Mendocino, 707-937-0104
  Mendosa's Merchandise & Market, 707-937-5879

Inverness offers Czechoslovakian dishes in the unusual and friendly atmosphere of Vladimir's Restaurant, 415-669-1021.

Barnaby's by the Bay offers a complete bar and wine list along with a tranquil view of the Tomales Bay at Inverness. Seafood is a specialty, 415-669-1114. mbryant@sonic.net

GREAT PLACES TO EAT

Bayview Restaurant at Inn At The Tides, excellent seafood selections and wine list. Their fish chowder is wonderful, 707-875-2751. http://www.wl.nezone.com

River's End is a cliff top restaurant overlooking the end of the Russian River in Jenner. Views, excellent food, cultural variety and color along with fresh, 707-865-2484.

Salt Point Lodge Bar and Grill has a fine chef. Open for breakfast. A solarium bar and spectacular ocean views. North of Jenner, 707-847-3238.

Tho an elegant Victorian setting, Little River Inn Restaurant is casual for breakfast or dinner. An excellent menu from swordfish to New York steak, 707-937-5942.

Hill House in Mendocino provides an elegant Victorian style with paintings and antiques. Enjoy seafood in an excellent setting above the ocean. Known for their great breakfasts, 707-937-0554.

In Ft. Bragg enjoy a brew at the North Coast Brewing Company. Excellent lunch selections in a relaxed atmosphere, 707-964-BREW http://www.ncoast-brew.com

SONOMA COUNTY

#3

DAY TRIP

TO

HEALDSBURG

ALEXANDER VALLEY

GEYSERVILLE

AND

CLOVERDALE

GREAT PLACES TO STAY

Honor Mansion B&B in Healdsburg is a delightful Victorian beautifully furnished in period pieces. Six rooms, pool, decks and a fine breakfast, 800-554-4667.

Madrona Manor is a 17 room Victorian with 8 acres of lawns and gardens, an excellent restaurant and fine reputation for quality service. 707-433-4231, May be seen on the internet at www.weddinglinks.com/

Calderwood Inn in Healdsburg is a very romantic B&B. This Victorian has magnificent decoration and gleaming wood. The fine dining room offers an excellent morning faire, 707-431-1110.

Camellia Inn a hospitable B&B is centered in Healdsburg. Within easy walking to the downtown square. Lovely rooms and well decorated to the period. A pool for those warm days and an excellent breakfast, 707-433-8182 or 800-727-8182.

A special honeymoon cottage will be found at Belle de Jour Inn. Set on a hill with views, a whirlpool, Franklin stove and king size bed. A full breakfast is served on the deck or in your room, 707-431-9777. They have four cottages.

Valhalla House is a pocket size estate with pool and several rooms for a group near Healdsburg. Pool, fully equipped kitchen and a view of Dry Creek Valley and the vineyards are part of the rental. 707-431-9757 - Mid Towne Realty

The new Geyserville Inn will offer twenty rooms, continental breakfast, pool and an excellent deli next door at the historic Hoffman House, 707-857-4343.

GREAT PLACES TO STAY

For a unique experience stay at the Isis Oasis. Everything from a pyramid to a yurt is offered to sleep in. An amazing collection of dwellings. Bodywork and massage available, 800-679-7387.

Ye Olde Shelford House in Cloverdale is one of the finest historic Queen Ann Victorians in the vineyards. The antiques and collections are outstanding. They offer six guest rooms, excellent breakfasts and tours in a 1929 Model A to the local wineries. An elegant retreat, 707-894-5956.

Vintage Towers B&B in Cloverdale has back yard gazebo, full breakfast, four rooms and three suites, 707-894-4535.

FUN THINGS TO DO

Windsor Water Slide, 700-838-7760.

Excellent shopping on Healdsburg Square.

The Historic Raven Theater brings first run movies to town.

Healdsburg is home to the well known Shoffeitt Seasoning Co. offers beautiful gift pack, 707-433-5555.

Formal Tea is served at the Healdsburg Inn on the Plaza. Call for reservations for this afternoon event, 707-433-6991.

The Sonoma County Wine Library houses history and wine related subjects in the Healdsburg branch of the library, 707-433-3772.

Outdoor Fun

Windsor's Hot Air Balloon Classic during the last week of June is a "must see" yearly event. The ground crews and lift off experience is a early morning breathtaking sight for all to see.

Beautiful Lake Sonoma and Warm Springs Damm are excellent for outdoor water sports, camping, hiking, picnicking and a visitors center with a salmon hatchery, 707-433-9483.

Canoeing on the Russian River from various points North of the Healdsburg Dam is available, there are many rentals available, 433-7247 local or 800-640-1386.

Ride the exciting train, Redwood Adventurer, through the vineyards North to Ukiah. A deli lunch or a gourmet lunch in the Dining Car or view from the Classic Dome car, 1-800-550-2122.

Rent a kayak at the California Rivers store in Windsor to go down the Russian River, 707-838-8919.

Aerostat Adventures originate from Piper Sonoma and Rodney Strong Vineyards over the Healdsburg valley, 800-579-0183.

Sonoma Thunder Balloon Safari for beautiful trips over the hills, valleys and vineyards, 707-996-3665.

Bicycle tours at the Spoke Folk Cyclery, 707-433-7171

Tayman Park Golf Course is a hilly and tough 9 hole par overlooking the beautiful Healdsburg Valley, 707-433-4275.

WINE TASTING

South of Healdsburg the Rodney Strong Winery, 707-431-1533 and Piper Sonoma, 707-433-8843 offer award winning wines and tours.

NorthEast of Healdsburg is along Hwy. 128 are the Sommer Winery and Alexander Fruit Company wines and beautiful gift packages of mustards, jams and sauces. Great summer concerts, 707-433-7209.

Fieldstone, Chalk Hill, Sausal and Johnson offer exceptional wines as does Murphy Goode and Hanna.

West of Healdsburg out Dry Creek to the dam be certain to stop at: Pezzi King Winery, Preston Vineyards, Robert Stremmler, Bellerose vineyard and Hop Klin. Many of these have picnic spots and spectacular views.

Dry Creek Vineyards serves Fumé Blanc and Zinfandel - excellent picnic spot, the Dry Creek General Store is nearby for the food.

Ferrari Carano Vineyards, Winery and Gardens. Plan to stroll, and enjoy the great gift shop in this extraordinary setting. Corporate events and concerts in the summer. Their wines include; Merlot, Sauvignon Blanc, Chardonnay and Fume Blanc, 707-433-6700.

Some of the most beautiful views of the area may be found close to the dam at Lake Sonoma Winery. Excellent wines including Chardonnay and Zinfandel are available. They serve gourmet picnic faire.

STORE MANIA

The Healdsburg Square is intended for strolling, quaint shops, bookstores, delightful coffee houses.

Kendall Jackson Wine Country Store includes cookbooks, glasses, and gourmet products along with excellent wine tastings.

Antiques are available throughout the area. Great finds for the small or large collector. Impressions Gallery has fine art and crafts 707-433-7510

WINE TASTING

Is incredible in this area! There are only a few named here but there are many wonderful wineries to explore.

In Healdsburg, visit the famous Simi Winery, Seghesio Winery, (by appointment) and the downtown Windsor Winery Tasting Room.

North along 101, you will find Trentadue Winery excellent wines including a port and marvelous picnic area, 707-433-3104.

Be certain to enjoy a stop at Chateau Souverain. A beautiful building and fine terraced cafe with spectacular views of vineyards and surrounding hillsides await you, 707-433-8268.

J. Pedroncelli Winery makes an exceptional Brut Rose. Tastings at Geyser Peak along with Canyon Road and Clos du Bois are in the area.

GREAT PLACES TO EAT

Giorgio's Restaurant is a 1913 Farmhouse at the South end of town offers Neapoloitan specialities. Full bar, patio amid waterfall and pond, 707-433-1106.

The tiny restaurant "Bistro Ralph" is a must do on the square. Get there early, it is a favorite with the locals.

The Rex in Geyserville is owned by the Catelli family. American-Italian dishes and great steaks are served inside or on the patio. An exceptional wine list is available for the Alexander Valley vintages, 707-433-6000.

GREAT PLACES TO EAT

Costeaux French Bakery is one of the greatest finds. Whether for lunch on the sidewalk, or a fancy cake for events....they have the touch, 707-433-1913.

Jimtown Intown is new and Healdsburg on the square and the Coffee Company Cafe offer great coffee and treats - lunches of salads, soups and specials.

Jimtown Store along Hwy 128 is great for morning coffee, espresso and coffee cake, excellent lunches for picnics. A patio for lunch and dinner beckons on warm summer evenings, 707-433-1212.

Breakfast and Lunch at the Charcuterie & Deli. Excellent and unusual menu selections, 707-431-7213.

The Bear Republic Micro Brewery offers a wide variety of brews. Excellent food for lunch or dinner and beautifully presented, Near the Healdsburg Square, 707-433-BEER.

Lunch or dinner at the Soutside Saloon on Healdsburg Square leads to an interesting and beautifully presented meal. Their wine list and beautiful bar make this an excellent choice, 707-433-4466.

Lunch or dinner on the Healdsburg Square at Western Boot Steak House. Plenty of room for large groups, 707-433-6362.

The historic Hoffman House in Geyserville for lunch and picnic fixings is a favorite spot, 707-857-3264.

Lake and Mendocino Counties

#4

DAY TRIP
INLAND TO
CLEARLAKE
BOONVILLE
HOPLAND
AND
WILLITS

GREAT PLACES TO STAY

These lovely areas are known for redwood groves, lumbering, fruit orchards and the ever growing wine industry. Champagne is at its best in the warmer valleys of these areas. Traquility is the essence of the forested hills. You will find the contrast of sofistication and blue jeans from people all around the world who have settled here.

Lake County

Konocti Harbor Resort and Spa has 250 units at Clearlake Deluxe apartments, and suites with kitchens are available. Lake sports, pools and tennis are available. Summer concerts by known rock and country stars are a favorite event. Sunday champagne brunch is a must, 800-862-4930. http://www.lakeresorts.com

Forbestown Inn is a 1863 B&B with four guest rooms. Victorian claw foot tubs, a library, garden, large pool and a hot tub are part of the delights. Excellent breakfast are offered and bicycles to work them off are available for local use, 707-263-7858.

Fetzer Vineyards offers a lovely B&B on the vineyard property in Hopland. The shaded and grassy lawns make this a park-like setting, A beautiful 3 acre organic garden is out the window, 707-744-1737. http://www.fetzer.com

Mendocino

In Hopland the Thatcher Inn is a picture out of a movie. The rooms are well appointed with antiques and decorated with style. A major hotel to the area from the 1890's for train and stage coach travelers, it has been restored with love. An excellent library and dinning area plus a beautiful long bar are part of the historic features of this 21 room hotel, 707-744-1890.

GREAT PLACES TO STAY

In Hopland, Fetzer Vineyards has a lovely B&B on the vineyard grounds in the original carriage house. Well decorated, both light and airy. The rooms and suites are available, some with whirpool baths and kitchens. 800-846-8637.

In Ukiah area, the historic Vichy Springs Resort is a true retreat. The 1854 mineral springs resort has health benefits for those who relax in the mineral baths and on the shaded lawns and by the swimming pool. Several cottages and rooms are available. Comfortably decorated. Massages are available, 707-462-9515.

In Boonville, the hotel has eight rooms with decor created by local artisans. Unusual, sparse, yet comfortable. Enjoy a continental breakfast in the dinning area or on the patio, 707-895-2210.

In Philo (near Hendy Redwoods), the delightful Philo Pottery Inn was a stagecoach stop. It has four guest rooms and a one room cottage with fireplace. 707-895-3069.

Fun Things to Do

See the Lake County Museum which includes Pomo Indian displays, collections of gems, musical instruments and local history. Museum is located in what was once the county courthouse, 707-263-4555.

Tour a Gold Mine in the Lakeport area. Homestake Mining Company is one of the few available for tours.

In Ukiah, enjoy the historic Grace Hudson Museum and the Sun House. Hudson was known for her Pomo Indian paintings. The museum holds paintings, local history and artifacts, 707-467-2836 for tour hours.

On Saturday mornings from May through October, the Boonville Farmers Market is a pleasure to experience. 9 a.m. to noon.

Outdoor Fun

The Clearlake Queen is a Mississippi paddlewheel boat touring Clearlake during the summer, 707-994-5432.

Rent a bike near Clearlake at the Bicycle Rack, 707-263-1200. Rental of jet skis for Clearlake are available at On The Waterfront, 707-263-6789.

Crazy Creek Gliders and Skydivers is located in Middletown. Schedule lessons or flights, 707-987-9393.

Outdoor Fun

Buckingham Golf and Country Club, 707-279-4863.
Clear Lake Riviera Golf Course, 707-277-7129.

Hendy State Park near Booneville offers campgrounds and trails through the 1,000 year old redwoods. Reservations must be made well in advance for this popular spot, 800-444-7275. www.destinate.com

Navarro River Redwood State Park is a dense redwood grove and campground, 707-937-5804. www.men.org/1/mendopark/mendo.htm

Montgomery Woods State Park has a trail through 700 acres of redwoods, 707-937-5804. www.men.org/1/mendopark/mendo.htm

WINE TASTING LAKE COUNTY

Konocti Winery is located in Kelseyville and offers Merlot, and an Semillon and Cabernet Franc. A shaded picnic area is available.

Guenoc Vineyards Estate and Winery is in Middletown. Lillie Langtry used this as a country retreat in the 1880's. The Victorian home is the tasting room. Several wines are poured; a Port, Petite Sirah, and several Chardonnays, 707-987-2385.

Horne Winery and Channing Rudd Cellars as well as Wildhurst Vineyards are in the general Middletown area, 707-987-3503.

Weible in Ukiah has taken on a new name and concept with many vintners sharing the large tasting room as the wine center.

WINE TASTING IN MENDOCINO

Scharffenberger Cellars in Philo produces a methode champenoise and three cuvees. Be certain to try Blanc de Blanc and Brut Rose. The beautiful grounds and 1,000 year old redwoods in the surrounding hills are awe inspiring, 800-824-7154 or 707-895-2065. avfizz@pacific.net

Wine Tasting in Mendocino

Fetzer Vineyards in Hopland offers my favorite Gewurztraminer and other fine Chardonnay and Cabernet Sauvignon. Brandy, grape juice, olive oils and gourmet food products along with picnic supplies are sold in the tasting room. All types of events and music are offered at this winery throughout the year. John Ash conducts classes for chefs. Be certain to tour the organic garden and have a picnic in the shaded patio area, 707-744-1737. http://www.fetzer.com

McDowell Valley Vineyards in Hopland offers Syrah, red table wines and several other unusual and difficult to grow varietal grape blends. Picnic and bbqs are available, 707-744-1774.

Dunnewood Vineyards and Winery in Ukiah produce Cabernet, Merlot, Gamay, Beaujolais and Zinfandel, 707-462-2987.

Parducci Wine Cellars is in the fourth generation of family wine production. North of Ukiah, they have a picnic area, 707-463-5350.

Redwood Valley Cellars offers daily tasting of the sparkling wines and A picnic and camping area are available, 707-485-0321.

Roederer Estate offers a lovely setting and award winning sparkling wines Christine Woods Winery, Husch Vineyards Handley Cellars and the Navarro Vineyards all have excellent reputations.

Greenwood Ridge Vineyards offers daily tasting but has hosted the California Wine Tasting Championships since 1983. During the last weekend in July wine flows with food, live music and sunshine, 707-895-2002. www.avwines.com

GREAT PLACES TO EAT

Park Place to Go will create a great picnic for you in Lakeport. 707-263-1033, or stay and enjoy pasta salad and a great sandwich.

In Kelseyville the Oak Barrel offers a varied menu of seafood, Cajun style recipes along with chicken, steak or lamb dishes. On Sunday night the seafood is excellent and includes oysters and mussels, 707-279-0101.

Hopland's Bluebird Cafe offers hearty breakfasts. The menu varies from vegetarian and fresh fruit to well prepared meats.

Hopland's Thatcher Inn offers Tuscan style menus with seafood and excellent deserts. Meals are served in a historic dining room or on the patio. Mystery theater on some evenings, 707-744-1890.

In Hopland the Mendocino Brewing Company was the first in 1980 to open a tavern at their brewery. Casual food and the famous Red Tail Ale is made here. Saturday evenings in the summer finds this spot rocking with blues to country, 707-744-1015. mendobrew.com

Your "sweet tooth" will be satisfied at the Cheesecake Lady's shop in Hopland. Croissants, danish and an extensive selection of cheesecakes, 707-744-1441. e mail cakelady@zapcom.net

The Boonville Restaurant and Bar is run by very talented chefs specializing in Southwestern cooking and Italian foods. Lunch and dinner in the summers. Reservations are recommended, 707-895-2210.

NAPA COUNTY

#5

DAY TRIPS
TO THE TOWNS OF
NAPA
YOUNTVILLE
AND
RUTHERFORD

GREAT PLACES TO STAY

The beautiful Napa area at the lower end of the valley has some of the finest Victorians, wineries, resorts and chefs in the world. A small port along the Napa River in the 1850's, it grew into a lovely city of tree-lined streets.

The Beazley House B&B was built in 1902. It has 10 large rooms well appointed with antiques and comfort, a garden, and an excellent breakfast is offered, 800-559-1649.

An extraordinary Colonial Revival mansion is the Churchill Manor. A full breakfast is served, they have exceptional weddings and receptions here and will reserve the entire site, 707-253-7733.

The Blue Violet Mansion in Napa has, by far, the most beautiful honeymoon suites in the area. This National award winning B&B offers special services including breakfast in your room, flower arrangements, picnic baskets, candlelight champagne dinners and massages, 707-253-BLUE.

Cedar Gables Inn is a B&B in Napa. It has excellent rooms in a historic home. The rooms look out on tree lined streets and cedar trees. The library, foyer, and lovely rooms are well appointed with antiques, 707-224-7969.

The Elm House is a modern, clean crisp in-town Inn. Comfort and hospitality are a plus in this moderately priced inn, 707-255-1831.

For larger groups the Napa Valley Marriotts Hotel located near the main highway has fine rooms with poolside gardens and two restaurants, 707-253-7433.

GREAT PLACES TO STAY

East of Napa, the Silverado Country Club and Resort offers cottages, condos, suites, houses with four bedrooms. A 18 hole golf course and 20 tennis courts, an excellent restaurant, plus vineyard views are all in this beautiful setting, 800-532-0500.

Vintage Inn is located in Yountville overlooking a vineyard. It affords easy walking distance throughout the town and lovely rooms with a romantic flair, 800-982-5539.

Auberge du Soleil sits atop a hill overlooking miles of vineyards in the Rutherford area. Cottages, gardens, a five star restaurant, and tennis courts make this an exceptional place, 800-348-5406.

Webber Place is a B&B in Yountville with a homey ranch feeling. Antique quilts, old fashioned tubs, front porch lounging, and several cottages , spa and swimming pool, 800-647-7177.

FUN THINGS TO DO

Napa Valley Wine Train has great food and exception wines for tasting as it winds through the valley. A 36 mile trip day or evening. Christmas is especially pretty with the twinkle lights on the cars. http://www.napavalley.com/winetrain, 800-427-4124.

Napa River Boat is a small paddle wheel which takes you up and down the Napa River serving lunch or dinner, 707-226-2628.

The Massage Place, by appointment in Yountville, 707-944-1387#3.

OUTDOOR FUN

Bonaventura Balloon Company brings you aloft in beautiful balloons over the vineyards serving champagne brunches, 707-944-2210.

Chimney Rock Golf Course is a 9 hole golf course, 707-255,3363.

Napa Municipal Golf Course is a 18 hole course and driving range. 707-255-4333.

Napa Valley Cyclery offers all types of bikes including tandems, head gear and tours, 800-707-BIKE.

Walking tour of the Victorians on the tree lined streets of Napa. Pick up a map at the Visitors Bureau in Napa Towne Center.

John's Rose Garden has 500 species of roses including historic varieties. May throughout summer blooms, 707-224-8002.

STORE MANIA

Grapevine Wreath Company just off the Silverado Trail has exceptional gifts made of grapevines, 707-226-7182.

Groezinger Wine Company will ship wines after you have selected them from their excellent tasting room, 707-944-2331.

If discount is your password, Napa's Discount Shopping Mall will give you excellent brand names and labels. Located West of the Freeway in Napa. This huge complex sports over thirty stores.

Spend a day immersed in Yountville 1870. Over forty shops in this historic brick building. The streets are lined with great stores and there are exceptional art galleries at Beard Plaza. Don't miss the train and caboose called Whistle Stop Center.

WINE TASTING

Not to be missed is the Montecillo Cellars in the center of the valley on Big Ranch Rd. The house looks like President Jeffersons. Chardonnay and Cabernet Sauvignons are served, 707-253-2802.

Pine Ridge along the Silverado Trail has terraced the hills with rows of grapes. Delightful gardens and a shady picnic area are available, 707-252-9777 or 800-575-9777.

S.Anderson Vineyards offer sparkling wines. A restful garden and daily tasting is available, 707-944-8642.

Also offering excellent champagne (sparkling wines) is Mumm Napa Valley. The gift store offers a wide selection of wine flutes and views of the Rutherford vineyards, 707-942-3400.

Robert Mondavi Winery offers so much to the public. Fine Cabernet, varietals and reserves, an excellent tasting and gift room, plus delightful summer concerts. Reserve your tour, 707-259-WINE. Check their web site at www.mondavi.com

Domaine Chandon is not to be missed. The tours educate on how sparkling wines are made, "methode champenoise." An excellent champagne museum and gardens are to be enjoyed. Across the highway from the Yountville 1870, 707-944-2280.

Sequoia Grove Vineyards between Rutherford and Oakville offer a delightful picnic spot with 100 year old redwoods, excellent Gewurztraminer and Cabernet Sauvignon, 707-944-2945.

GREAT PLACES TO EAT

Coffee houses abound Napa Valley Traditions and NV Coffee Roasting

Great coffee, Breakfast or Lunch in Napa at Alexis Baking Company and Cafe, 707-258-1827.

Gourmet Picnics for honeymooners or any picnic fantasy can be prepared by the Oakville Grocery Store, 800-736-6602.

Delightful picnics are created by Palmetto's Deli in Oakville, 707-944-2365.

Downtown Joe's in Napa has a great lunch and dinner setting along the Napa River. Great selection of beers, and homemade rootbeer along with outdoor seating, 707-258-2337.

Great places to eat in Napa to Oakville: River City in Napa is open for lunch or dinner. Steaks, pasta and sea food are offered in a pleasant setting, 707-253-1111.

The Villa Romano located South of Napa brings a Victorian home into great use. Italian faire, and plenty of it, 707-252-4533.

The Yountville Pastry Shop located at Vintage 1870 has delightful coffee, pastry and lunches. Patio dining available, 707-944-2138.

Lunch or dinner at Domaine Chandon Restaurant is exceptional. Patio or candle light and romance await in this lovely restaurant. Reservations for lunch or dinner are recommended. Jackets for evening required, 707-944-2892. dchadon@napanet.net

GREAT PLACES TO EAT

Compadres Bar & Grill offers a Mexican menu in a historic setting. 707-944-2406. http://www.wine.com/compadres

Piatti in Yountville has excellent food. A variety of Italian faire and Mediterranean specialties, 707-944-2070.

Mustard's Grill is the "locals hangout" offering lunch and dinner. A great bar and California style menu. Located in Yountville, they offer wonderful deserts. Reservations recommended, 707-944-2424.

Stars Oakville Cafe offers herbs and fresh vegetables in a variety of excellent recipes. Patio seating near gardens, 707-944-8905.

SONOMA COUNTY

#6

DAY TRIP
TO
ROHNERT PARK
AND
PETALUMA

GREAT PLACES TO STAY

The Double Tree Hotel in Rohnert Park, 800-547-8010.

Valley Ford Hotel - is a small private country hotel with hot tub West of Petaluma, 1-800-696-6679, excellent food and a peaceful setting. Basque restaurant in the area and near the coastal restaurants.

Golterman Gardens is a quiet B&B located within acres of gardens in the Petaluma area, 707-762-1761

FUN THINGS TO DO

The new California Visitors Review Center encompasses the Sonoma County Convention Bureau and the Wine Center. Located in Rohnert Park off Hwy. 101. This is a great place to embark upon your exploration of the wine country, 707-938-0780.

Cruise the Petaluma River on the Petaluma Queen, 800-750-7501

Petaluma is the Antique capital of the county. Stroll the old downtown area and see an eye-full of historic buildings. There are maps available to you from the Chamber for walking tours of the quaint Victorian homes.

Outdoor Fun

Mt. Shadow's Golf Course, 707-584-7766.

The Garden Valley Ranch has a self-guided and group tours of the rose gardens, 707-795-0919.

Sonoma / Marin Fair is held in Petaluma - June, 707-763-0931.

World Champion Wrist Wrestling - October 707-778-1430.

Store Mania

The Petaluma Mill near the downtown area is great for seeing unusual items and fun restaurants.

Antique Shops are along the Main Street of the old downtown area.

Petaluma has the new Village Factory Outlet with more than thirty name brands North end of town, 707-778-9300.

GREAT PLACES TO EAT

Lunch or dinner at Graziano's Ristorante 707-762-5997.

Lunch or dinner at Dempsey's Brewery, 707-765-9694.

Volpi's Italian for lunch or dinner. This historic building is the oldest speak-easy in Petaluma, 707-765-0695

Sunday Brunch at Sonoma Joe's

SONOMA COUNTY

#7

DAY TRIPS
TO THE
RUSSIAN RIVER
AND
OCCIDENTAL
AREA

GREAT PLACES TO STAY

This beautifully forested area is renowned for its apples, vineyards and redwoods. The Russian River moves toward the Pacific Ocean creating beautiful views and lovely picnic spots. The country tranquility and layed back charm has provided a playground for thousands each year. Known also for jazz festivals and the Bohemian Club's summer retreat. The hotels are hard to find, motels occasionally but a desire for Bed and Breakfasts is met at many turns in the Russian River area.

Nestled in the vineyards is The Farm House Inn and Restaurant at 707-887-3300 and The Raford House which has seven guest rooms at 800-887-9503. Both of these lovely buildings have views and gardens.

An exceptional and romantic Applewood B&B has 16 rooms, romantically decorated, pool and wooded, 707-865-2683

Huckleberry Springs has cottages on 56 acres, pool and spa, full breakfast, 800-822-2683.

Ridenhour Ranch House is near the Korbel Winery. They have gardens, great food and a hot tub, 707-887-1033.

On the Russian River, the Rio Villa Beach Resort in Monte Rio, it has cabins, decks and trees trees trees, 707-865-1143.

Heading into the Occidental area you will find the extraordinary Inn at Occidental. The Victorian handles small elopements and honeymooners, 800-522-6324.

On the ridge of forest above Occidental is the Golden Apple Ranch, homey, quiet and truly a refuge, 707-874-3756. You can see forever from the decks.

WINE TASTING

Martinelli Winery offers a variety of wines (check out the wine based chocolate sauces), 800-346-1627 and the Z Moore Wineries 707-544-3555 are located next door to one another along River Rd.

Another wine tasting nearby is Villa Pompei at 5800 River Rd. A fine view, beautiful plantation style mansion is located at 5800 River Rd, 707-545-5800.

In Forestville, Topolos, 707-887-1575 is next door to the famous Kozlowski Raspberry Farms (be certain to stop).

Nearby sample the wonderful wines of Iron Horse in Sebastopol, 707-887-1507 they have an excellent Wedding Cuve'.

Martini & Prati is one of the oldest wineries in Sonoma County they may be called for tasting schedule at 707-823-2404.

Sonoma Cutrer off River Road at 4401 Slusser Rd has one of the many championship croquet courses in the world. Their excellent wines may be tasted by appointment only, 707-528-1181.

West on River Rd. is the Korbel Winery (champagne), with historic rose gardens and an excellent living history museum. There are continuous tours throughout the week. 13250 River Rd, 707-887-2294.

STORE MANIA

Duncan Mills, toward the end of the Russian River has many quaint stores. Back To Entertaining is especially fun, 707-865-1155.

The historic logging town of Occidental has restaurants and shops. When in Occidental retreat to the nearby Osmosis Spa in Freestone.

Downtown Sebastopol is full of great shops, to explore.

Outdoor Fun

Nearby Sebastopol's Wine Country Carriages offer romantic carriage rides and gourmet picnics, 800-500-7083.

Great Golf Course is at Northwood's Golf Course at 707-865-1116.

Hiking trails up Austin Creek from Armstrong Grove.

In the summer it is fun to rent a canoe and travel down the Russian River. Several places in Guerneville will rent canoes.

Eagle Enterprise Tours of vineyards or coast, 707-546-9778.

River swimming and canoeing or laying on the beach along the Russian River at Johnson's Beach Resort, 707-869-2022.

Armstrong Redwood Grove is a preserve of the most beautiful Redwood Giants. You may walk, picnic and learn in this breathtaking park.

Great Places to Eat

Sunday Brunch or dinner at Cazanoma Lodge toward the end of Russian River 707-632-5255 has a romantic waterfall and deck for enjoyment.

Blue Heron at Duncan Mills has received awards for their fine foods, 707-865-9135.

Topolos Restaurant at the Russian River Vineyards, 707-887-1562. The summer patio dining is very romantic!

Chez Peyo - Sebastopol is a noted French chef, 707-823-1262. Lace curtains, cozy and romantic.

Union Hotel and Garden - Occidental, 707-823-1717

SONOMA COUNTY

#8

DAY TRIPS

TO

SANTA ROSA

AREA

GREAT PLACES TO STAY

Santa Rosa is the county seat for Sonoma County. A community in itself with symphony, cultural and sports events. Being in the heart of the wine country, the city attracts thousands of visitors each year.

The historic LaRose Hotel on Railroad Square offers beautiful rooms with antiques, 707-579-3200.

The Hilton (formerly the Doubletree) in Santa Rosa sits on a hill overlooking the city. Lovely terrace and good dining plus the rooms are light, fresh and furnished well, 707-523-7555.

The Gables B&B is located at the South end of Santa Rosa on Petaluma Hill Rd. A romantic Victorian, 707-585-7777.

Vintner's Inn is a 44 room European style luxury accommodation North of Santa Rosa adjacent to the vineyards, 707-575-7350.

The Flamingo Resort Hotel has a beautiful setting with pool, gym and tennis courts in the heart of Santa Rosa, 707-545-8530.

Fun Things to Do

Explore the "Snoopy's Gallery and Gift Store located at the Redwood Empire Ice Rink. This is where Charles Schultz's characters are found. Original drawings, prints, gifts, and loveable characters of Snoopy, Peanuts, Linus and Lucy are available. (Be certain to go upstairs for the special displays). 1667 W. Steele Lane, 707-546-7147

Two great museums are Robert Ripley's Memorial Museum 707-524-5233 and the Sonoma County Museum 707-579-1500. The Santa Rosa Junior Native American Art Museum on the campus, 707-527-4479.

Luther Burbank's home and gardens is located at 204 Santa Rosa Ave. His world renowned horticultural genius brought us shasta daisy, Santa Rosa plums, russet potatoes. His gardens are beautiful and the blooms are ever changing, 707-524-5445.

Store Mania

Walking downtown Fourth Street and enjoying the interesting and varied shops is great. Most are open on Thursday evenings. The restaurants have a bistro sidewalk flair. Farmers Market is Thursday evenings in the summer.

Railroad Square offers antique shops, art, restaurants and music.

Montgomery Village in the East end of town has an exciting variety of style shops along with art, books and culinary interests. The gardens are enjoyable throughout the year.

In Montgomery Village, Clo's IceCream and memorbilia of their delightful cartoons in gift styles, 707-545-6000.

WINE TASTING

Cheateau DeBaun is Kendal Jackson's fine wine tasting and event site at the North End of Santa Rosa on Fulton is a beautiful setting with gardens and excellent wines, 707-544-4400.

Paradise Ridge Winery sits high above the city for spectacular views, 707-528-9463

Chateau St. Jean winery and gardens are East toward the town of Sonoma on Hwy. 12. 707-833-4134

Southeast in Bennett Valley is the Matanzas Creek Winery at 6097 Bennett Valley Rd., 707-528-6464. Hanna Winery has Occidental Rd. tasting room in the West Santa Rosa area 707-575-3371.

Outdoor Fun

Rincon Cyclery at 4927 H Sonoma Hwy. 12 and Middle Rincon will rent you bikes to enjoy the many beautiful parks nearby, 800-965-BIKE

Howarth City Park is great for walks, biking, and children's playground. This park adjoins a regional park called Spring Lake. Fishing, boating, windsurfing, walking and biking pathways are a plus in this beautiful setting.

Other nearby parks are Annadel, and Hood Mountain, 707-576-2186.

Great golf courses are: Fountaingrove Country Club 707-579-4653, Windsor Golf Course 707-838-PUTT, and Bennett Valley Golf Course.

Farmer's Market is in full swing on Thursday evenings downtown on Fourth Street during summer and fall. Fresh produce and a variety of foods to try.

Parades and Festivals: Rose Parade - May.

Sonoma Harvest Fair - Early October.

June 28th & 29th - Hot Air Balloon Classic in Windsor 707-575-6555.

Pillow Fights in Kenwood, 4th of July.

Sonoma County Fair and Quarter Horse races 3rd & 4th week of July

GREAT PLACES TO EAT

Coffee houses abound in Santa Rosa, Wolfs, Aroma Roasters and the Sonoma Coffee Co, plus a few drive through Expresso/Coffee spots.

Breakfast at The Omelette Express on Railroad Square, 707-525-1690

Lunch or dinner at Michelle's on Railroad Square is plentyful, but Sunday Brunch is abundant. 707-542-2577

Lunch or dinner at Mixx on Railroad Square serves healthy California cuisine and stays open late to serve extraordinary deserts by Kathleen. Their wine lists include many of the Sonoma County Harvest Fair winners, 707-573-1344

The Renaissance Pastry at 525 Mendocino Ave (downtown) 707-544-2253, are Sonoma Harvest Fair award winning and wonderful. Your sweet tooth will find confections beyond belief. Excellent wedding cakes.

Picnic Lunches at Mixx Express in Railroad Square 707-573-5845.

Picnic Lunches at Tote Cuisine in Montgomery Village 707-578-0898.

Lunch at Michelle Marie's Patisserie in Montgomery Village is a combination of soups, salads and great sandwiches…not to speak of their wonderful desert items, 707-575-1214

Lunch or Dinner at Cattlemens gives steak a real meaning, 707-545-6000. Crisp salads, bbq beans and a varied menu are a plus.

Lunch or Dinners at the downtown Mexican Cantina, 707-523-3663. A festive patio flavor with a downtown atmosphere.

GREAT PLACES TO EAT

Lunch or Dinner at Cá Bianca is one of Santa Rosa's newest and best. Gaining rave revues examples the hard work to restore this historic Victorian house. Excellent Italian Faire, 707- 542-5800.

Josef's Restaurant at the LaRose Hotel offers a intimate setting and an excellent variety of food and wine menu, 707-571-8664.

La Grande's Trattoria has a country atmosphere to relax, enjoy and stay awhile - Italian Faire, 707-584-880.

Mark West Restaurant - offers fresh seafood, several flamed preparations, duck, steak and lobster, 707-528-0999

Clo's Ice Cream - Montgomery Village offers ice cream and Clo's cartooned shirts and logo items.

[#]9

DAY TRIPS

TO

SAN FRANCISCO

GREAT PLACES TO STAY

Though not in the vineyards, you may have a days stay in San Francisco on the honeymoon agenda or for you or guests while in the area. A dreaded flight delay can turn into fun with this. One day in San Francisco would hardly touch the surface of this beautiful city, but these are a few spots you may include while visiting this jewel on the bay.

The Archbishop's Mansion B&B - 800 543-5820 - Elegant Victorian.

Edward II B&B - 5 suites have whirlpools - 415-922-3000.

The Amsterdam Hotel B&B - 800-637-3444 - 1906 Victorian Hotel.

Hyatt at Fisherman's Wharf - 415-563-1234.

Cathedral Hill Hotel - 415-776-8200 - excellent views.

The historic Palace Hotel - 800-325-3589 - 550 rooms.

FUN THINGS TO DO

Ride the cable cars, and visit the cable room.

Explore the DeYoung Museum which houses and displays the finest San Francisco art exhibits plus touring exhibits in the world.

Don't miss Fort Point (right under the Golden Gate Bridge).

If you love seeing how things work, you will enjoy the Exploratorium Museum at the Palace of Fine Arts.

Enjoy the shops and art along the streets and stores of China Town.

The theater district offers a variety of plays including Phantom of the Opera. They may have a cancelation are order ahead at Bass Ticket office.

OUTDOOR FUN

Walk or ride a bike across the Golden Gate Bridge is a fresh air experience.

Experience the beautiful Golden Gate Park and the variety of gardens and displays from windmills to Japanese Tea Gardens.

Take the Larkspur Ferry across the San Francisco Bay to Marin and back. No views are similar to the ones of the bridges and islands from being on the water.

Store Mania Ghiradelli Square and Pier 39 are must sees. They become a tourists dream when you add Fisherman's Wharf.

Par elegance, do not miss Gumps Department Store on St. Francis Square. (it houses art and tasteful gifts). You can park under St.Francis Square.

GREAT PLACES TO EAT

"Fact" There are 3500 restaurants in S.F.

Coffee Houses, Bagels and Bakeries abound in San Francisco.

Lunch or Dinner at the Cliff House - has views of the Pacific Ocean and the funky Musee' Mecanique amusement arcade make this a must, 415-386-3330.

Lunch at the Neiman Marcus "Rotunda" 415-362-4777, 11 am - 5:00 pm.

China Town is great for lunch or dinner - many excellent spots.

Elegant Dinners at Wu Kon Shanghai Restaurant, 415-957-9300.

Fish dinners, pasta, steaks, and Bay Views at McCormick & Kuleto's at Ghiradelli Square, 415-929-1730.

Alioto's at Fishermans Wharf 415-673-0183, fishing boat views.

Carnelian Room - Continental Cuisine - 52 stories above the city 415-433-7500 - what a view!

Ghiradelli Square offers a unforgettable sweets shop for indulgent hot fudge sundae fans. (Suggest you skip a meal for this).

SONOMA COUNTY

#10

DAY TRIPS
TO THE
TOWN OF
SONOMA
GLEN ELLEN
AND
KENWOOD

GREAT PLACES TO STAY

Over 13,000 acres of vineyards grow in the Valley of the Moon. The Sonoma Valley is prime viticulture region and the historic home of the California wine industry. Glen Ellen was home to famous author Jack London. The famous drive along Highway 12 East to Sonoma is full of wonderful wineries to explore.

Relais du Soleil is a B&B tucked back on a quiet road along a stream, 707-833-6264. A ranch house with bunk house, deck, and several rooms for guests.

Kenwood Inn and Spa is a formidable Italian Villa in view of the vineyards. They provide a pool and health spa with massage, fireplaces and private baths, 800-353-6966 or 707-963-1211.

Gaige House in Glen Ellen brings Victorian grace, hospitality and excellent breakfasts to their guests, 800-935-0237. They host culinary classes.

The El Dorado Hotel, located on Sonoma Town Square has 26 rooms and a restaurant and heated pool, 800-289-3031.

Sonoma Mission Inn is historic, elegant and has a mineral water health spa, pool, restaurant and tennis, 707-939-2467.

The Sonoma Hotel has 17 rooms on three floors, a foyer with lace curtains and antiques in every room, 800-468-6016. The restaurant provides international cusine and a fun Sunday Brunch.

Fun Things to Do

Visit the Mission and historic buildings on the square in Sonoma The Train Museum holds fascination for young and old alike. Visit Historic General Vallejo's home.

See a play and have a box dinner or bring your picnic to Jack London State Park Vineyard Theater. 707-585-7883

Outdoor Fun

Oakmont Golf Course 707-538-2454 and Sonoma Golf Course.

Hiking Sugar Loaf State Park trails is a favorite. Redwood, fir, oak and chaparral give way to 25 miles of hiking trails. There are 50 campsites and has trails leading to Hood Mountain Regional Park 800-444-7275 for information or reservations.

Explore the book store and Wolf House at Jack London St. Park in Glen Ellen 707-938-5216. Reprints of Londons work's and his history will be found here.

Aero Schellville airplane rides, 707-778-6767.

Sonoma Thunder Wine Country Balloon Safaris, 800-759-5638 or 707-538-7359.

Air Flamboyant Hot Air Balloons, 800-456-4711 or 707-838-8700.

Store Mania

The wine Exchange of Sonoma hosts 500 California wines, 250 beer brews and knowledge about selecting both for gifts. A unique store which will ship your purchases, 800-938-1794.

Sonoma Jack Cheese Factory has excellent tasting of jack, mild cheddar and Teleme and gift baskets, 707-996-1931.

Viansa's Italian Marketplace at the Viansa Winery serves some of the finest wines, but has one of the most unique (marketplaces), 707-935-4700.

Wine Tasting

Landmark Winery in Kenwood is known for their beautiful events as well as their Chardonnay. The lovely grounds are great for a picnic, 707-833-0053.

Wine Tasting at Kunde Estate Winery is a remarkable experience. Fountains and water pools under the oaks with hillsides of vineyards in every direction. The specialize in Chardonnay, Merlot and Zinfandel, 707-833-5501.

Benziger Family Winery gives you the "hands on experience" in Glen Ellen. The interactive tram tour is very informative as you drive out through the vineyard, 707-935-4046.

Gloria Ferrer Champagne Caves brings a touch of Spain. Tour man made caves and taste some of the finest wines and champagne from this awesome setting on the hillside overlooking vineyards. 707-707-996-7256.

GREAT PLACES TO EAT

Breakfast coffee and fresh breads and pastry are served at the Sonoma French Bakery on the Town Square, 707-996-2691.

Lunch or dinner is served at Cafe Citti on Hwy. 12, in Kenwood, 707-833-2690. (They can make you a marvelous picnic).

Lunch or dinner at the Kenwood Restaurant and Bar is enjoyable. It has an open patio and excellent food, 707-833-6326. Closed M-Tu.

The historic Generals Daughter is a "must" for excellent food at a beautiful setting in this restored Victorian.

Picnics by Lainie's Cuisine to Go 707-996-5226. Elaine Bell has made her reputation by serving excellent foods at catered events. We are able to partake of a few of her recipes here.

Lunch or dinner at the historic Depot Hotel Restaurant and Garden Italian flair in this lovely historic setting, 707-938-2980

Lunch or dinner at La Casa is a step into Mexican history. Enjoy the patio and favorites from Marguerites to Flan, 707-996-3406.

ADVERTISERS

DIRECTORY

PROFESSIONALS

AT THEIR

BEST

CA'BIANCA

Romantic Gardens and Patio
for Weddings and Receptions
Rehearsal Dinners
Private Banquet Rooms 25
Contact for Wedding Karin Hoehne
707-542-5800

PRESS DEMOCRAT ★ ★ ★ ★

MARIN INDEPENDENT ★ ★ ★ ↓
"one of 10 best new restaurants in bay area"

CHRONICAL "One of 3 Best
Moderate Priced Restaurants in Bay Area"

Mountain Shadows
GOLF RESORT

Your wedding reception or ceremony
will overlook our beautiful golf
courses. Perfect for an intimate
rehearsal dinner or an elaborate
celebration. Please call our on-site
coordinator for a tour of
Mountain Shadows Golf Resort

707-584-9797

100 Golf Course Drive • Rohnert Park

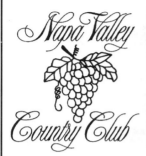

NOTES

Relais du Soleil
A Wine Country Guest Ranch

Weddings, Bachelor Receptions, Small Intimate Gatherings, 120 acres, Au Natural, at the base of the Macayamas Mountain Range in Sonoma County, Relais du Soleil is minutes from all major wineries, yet private & intimate & quiet.

Relais du Soleil, French for... "A place to rest in the Sun" is nestled in Nuns Canyon in Glen Ellen. Glen Ellen was the home of Jack London famous for his writings in the late 1800's. Relais du Soleil, a turn-of-the-century, Country Farm House & Guest Ranch is situated in the heart of the Wine Country, just 10 minutes from historical downtown Sonoma and minutes from the Valley of the Moon's famous wineries & fine restaurants.

1210 Nuns Canyon Road, Glen Ellen, California 95442

Tel: 707-833-6264   Fax: 707-833-6151
E. Mail: soleil@sonic.net

Elegant Occasions

Extraordinary Foods Created
in an Elegant Victorian Setting

- Romantic Dinners for Two
- Rehearsal Dinners
- Receptions ~ Celebrations

400 W. Spain Street, Sonoma, California 95476

707-938-4004

NOTES

NOTES

Wedding Gowns
Brides Maids Gowns
Invitations & Accessories
Wedding Coordinating

Weddings by Darlene

WEDDINGS IN THE MENDOCNINO WINE COUNTRY

by
Deborah Kanani

Many couples are discovering the beauty and romantic qualities of bringing their weddings, receptions and honeymoons to the Mendocino County. Just a few hours north of the Golden Gate Bridge you will find an abundance of lovely wineries, redwood settings and the Pacific Coast locations filled with romance for your wedding or honeymoon.

Couples are in a traveling wedding trend. Families meet from all over the world in one spot for a wedding. Many people are amazed at the services and locations found in what was once thought of as a remote area of the U.S. We find top professionals running many of the establishments, chefs from excellent backgrounds plus wine and champagne makers from around the world who have ensconced themselves in these beautiful locations. They bring extraordinary talent to a pristine area of beauty.

Most wedding locations require a wedding consultant. That consultant will have first hand knowledge of the professionals in the area. The consultant's evaluation of the professionals and locations in the area will include helping you understand how each does business, saving you time and allowing your event to run smoothly.

The Mendocino enticement is to couple s seeking something environmental and unique for their wedding or honeymoon. All are part of the Mendocino area. From spring through the colorful autumn in the vineyards, romance is alive in this varied and beautiful county.

Extraordinary Wedding Desserts By

MEG SMITH PHOTOGRAPHY

Perfect Endings

Where the way your wedding cake tastes matters.

NAPA VALLEY
(707) 259-0500

SAN FRANCISCO BAY AREA
(510) 724-4365

Complimentary Tasting and Consultation by Appointment

R A V E   R E V I E W S

An Independent Evaluation of Perfect Endings

"The best pastry chefs in the Bay Area. I've seen it all and they are the best... cakes and deserts spectacularly presented"

"Excellent quality, high standards, premium ingredients... finally wedding cakes that taste as good as they look!"

"Courteous, reliable, detail oriented... they have mastered the art of 'Simple Elegance' with picture perfect cakes... in taste and presentation they are without peer"

"Innovative, consistent, superb... there is nobody better at wedding cakes"

QUOTES WERE EXCERPTED FROM MULTIPLE INTERVIEWS
WITH EVENT INDUSTRY PROFESSIONALS BY AN
INDEPENDENT MARKETING COMPANY

For the Perfect Wine Country Wedding
Award Winning Haute Patisserie

Consultation & Tasting by Appointment Only

525 Mendocino Avenue • Santa Rosa • 707-544-CAKE

Modern Sensibility
with old world craft

XXI

21ST CENTURY PASTRY

141 Petaluma Blvd.
Petaluma, CA
94952

707.763.2100

NOTES

Serving couples since 1972 with
professionalism, style and elegance

Mediterranean, Asian, Italian, Californian Cuisine
Formal, Theme, BBQ's
Equipped to "Party" Anywhere

Our role as caterer is to be sure that your event
runs smoothly from planning to completion.

128 Carlos Drive, Ste. A, San Rafael, CA 94903

415-472-4484

Please feel free to call us, for a complimentary consultation.

OUI CATER

A PREMIER SONOMA COUNTY CATERER
FEATURING CUSTOM TAILORED MENUS
OF THE FRESHEST AND FINEST FOODS
PRESENTED WITH
A WINE COUNTRY FLAIR

707   431·8355

A Lady Minister
Rev. Janine Vashio & Associates
Wedding Ceremonies

Beautiful ceremonies of varying length
Suited to your preference and style

Location of your choice, Including
the unique and adventurous

Nondenominational
Male and Female
Ministers

No church
affiliation
necessary

INTRODUCING
· Passions ·
of the Heart
An Adventurous Guidebook
for Designing Wedding
Celebrations
ORDER YOUR
COPY
TODAY

Call to reserve your date!
800~948~4849

The Wedding Belles

Jean Priestley-Rouas   Susan C. Smith

Ministers for a Unique Wedding Ceremony

We are non-denominational ministers whose purpose is to make certain that your special day is a dream come true. We work together as a unit; one officiates at the ceremony while the other organizes the wedding party. We are also available to act as consultants for your wedding.

P.O. Box 2422, Yountville, California 94599

707-944-9361

Hearts Desire
Chocolates

- ♥ Custom Chocolates
- ♥ Gift Baskets & Wedding Favors
- ♥ Sugar Free Chocolates and Fudge
- ♥ Unique Bridal Party Gifts
- ♥ Gold Coins
- ♥ Fresh Cream & Butter Fudge
- ♥ Imprinting & Shipping

"We Fit Your Budget!"
Located in the Double Tree Plaza

1-800-987-8333
707-795-7337 • 707-585-7673
707-586-0625 fax

NOTES

Call Our

Recommendation

Number

707-570-0820

Anguilla
WEST INDIES

Welcome to Anguilla, British West indies, where everyone is your host. From children to adults, faces are welcoming, people are friendly.

Dining on Angulla ... the piéce de résistance. French, Italian, Caribbean, Belgian, Creole, English, and American cuisine. Creatively prepared, attractively presented, graciously serve, thoroughly enjoyed.

Anguilla, every vacationer's dream. Exquisitely unique resorts, resplendent with architectural themes including Moroccan, Mediterranean, West Indian, Moorish.

Divers in Angullian waters explore reefs and wrecks. Snorkelers and divers enjoy the colorful and exotic marine life. Watersports enthusiasts waterski, windsurf and sail.

The national sport of Angulla is boat racing. Boats dot the sea during Carnival and on holidays.

Anguilla is surrounded by off-shore cays. Sail to Robinson Crusoe islands, enjoy lazy days of swimming, snorkeling, picnicking.

Renowned for its thirty miles of beautiful, pristine white sand beaches meeting crystal clear blue waters. Crescent shaped, horseshoe shaped, gently curved, lined by cliffs, edged by sea grapes. Anguilla welcomes you.

For more information or a brochure call
1-800-553-4939

V I N E Y A R D S

BED AND BREAKFAST

FOR ROMANTIC WEDDINGS AND HONEYMOONS

SET IN THE VINEYARDS OF MENDOCINO

THE CARRIAGE HOUSE AWAITS YOU

Ahhhh

Anguilla
British West Indies

BEACH FOUNTAIN BEACH

1-809-497-3491

Hi Sis,

Thanks for all your help with the wedding! Fountain Beach & Tennis Club is "perfect for a honeymoon". We are right on the reef and beach. The diving is fantastic! Miles of white sand – great food and the people are wonderful. So happy we found this spot in the Caribbean. Don't want to leave.

Love Teri

H M S
T R A V E L

NOTES

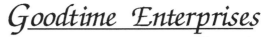

NOTES

NOTES

NOTES

NOTES

Film, Fashion,
Photography
and Bridal Artist

Wedding Day
Makeovers
"On Location"

Specializing in
Waterproof Eyes,
Kissproof Lips and
Custom Blended
Foundation

Hair and Nails
also Available

Jacqueline Scott
MAKE-UP ARTIST

Amici Studio
10 Fourth Street · Suite 103 · Santa Rosa
707.579.2611 or 707.575.9562

Michael B. Buchanan

Treasured Images ~ Artistically
& Joyfully Created since 1983

PHOTOGRAPHY

707-824-9751

Eileen Fahy
Event Photography

Romantic Images
by an Award Winning
Photojournalist

(707) 647-0420

Michael Loeb
PHOTOGRAPHY

FROM THE
SPONTANEOUS
AND IMAGINATIVE TO
THE FORMAL WEDDING…
MICHAEL LOEB TREATS
YOUR SPECIAL MOMENTS
WITH ARTISTIC FLAIR

(415) 453-8755

http://www.plexal.com/loeb

"Winning Photo
1995 Edition"

Margretha Lane Photography

WEDDING SPECIALIST

AND

LIFE STYLE PORTRAIT ARTIST

707 255-2234

Joshua B. Rotsten

QUALITY WEDDING

PHOTOGRAPHY

REASONABLY PRICED

TO FIT YOUR

BUDGET

P.O. BOX 121 ~ PETALUMA
CALIFORNIA 94953

707-762-4951

"After You've Experienced It, You'll Know Why!!!"

Brand New Stretch and Super-Stretch Limousines
Executive Sedan Service, Super Ultra-Stretch Limousines
Tuxedoed, Professional Chauffeurs, Premium Champagne
and Wet Bar, Wedding Decorations and Red Carpet Service
and most of all…
"FIRST CLASS SERVICE"

Since your Wedding is So Important
Call The Professionals!!!

Sonoma	(707) 795-1615
Marin	(415) 897-6255
San Francisco	(415) 485-1764
Napa	(707) 253-0296
Solano/Sacramento	(707) 425-4000
Worldwide Transportation	(800) 626-5466

Fully Insured and State Licensed TCP 7498 B

Carriage Occasions

- ✰ *Red Carpet Treatment*
- ✰ *Arabian Horses*
- ✰ *Antique Carriages*
- ✰ *Safe & Reliable*
- ✰ *Drivers Formally Attired*

707-546-2568

Ted & Nancy Draper
530 Irwin Lane, Santa Rosa, CA 95401

NOTES

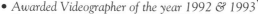

NOTES

ADVERTISERS DIRECTORY

LOCATIONS FOR WEDDINGS RECEPTIONS & REHEARSAL DINNERS NEARBY THE VINEYARDS

Ca Bianca Restaurant
835 2nd Street
Santa Rosa, CA
707-542-5800
page 257

Commodore Cruises
Port of Alemeda
weddings, receptions
and rehearsal dinners
Ward and Susan Proescher
Lafayette, CA
510-256-4000
page 258

Madrona Manor
Historic Inn
1001 Westside Road
Healdsburg, CA
707-433-4231
page 259

Mark West Restaurant
2520 Mark West Springs Rd.
Santa Rosa, CA
707-528-0999
page 260

Mt. Shadows Golf Resort
100 Golf Course Dr.
Rohnert Park, CA
707-584-9797
page 261

Napa Valley Country Club
3385 Hagen Road
Napa, CA
707-252-1111
page 262

Relais Du Soleil
1210 Nuns Canyon Road
Glen Ellen, CA
707-833-6264
page 263

The General's Daughter
400 West Spain Street
Sonoma, CA
707-938-4004
page 264

BRIDAL APPAREL

Brides and Maids
621 College Ave
Santa Rosa, CA
707-545-2772
page 265

Weddings by Darlene
Napa Town Center
Napa, CA
707-255-4161
page 267

ADVERTISERS DIRECTORY

BRIDAL CONSULTANTS

A Dream Wedding
Robbin Montero
Santa Rosa, CA
707-762-0882
page 266

Mendocino Weddings
Deborah Kanani
P.O. Box 211
Comptche, CA
707-937-1140
page 268-69

Weddings by Darlene
Napa Town Center
Napa, CA
707-255-4161
page 267

CAKES

21st Century
141 Petaluma Blvd.
Petaluma, CA
707-763-2100
page 272

Perfect Endings
Napa, 707-259-0500
S.F. Bay Area, 510-724-4365
page 270

Renaissance Pastry
525 Mendocino Avenue
Santa Rosa, CA
707-544-CAKE
page 271

CATERER

Creative Catering
128 Carlos Suite A
San Rafael, CA
415-472-4484
page 273

Oui Cater
Randi Middleton
Healdsburg, CA
707-431-8355
page 274

ADVERTISERS DIRECTORY

CLERGY

A Lady Minister Association
Rev. Janine Vashio
non-denominational ministers
Rohnert Park, CA
707-585-7575
800-948-4849
page 275

The Wedding Belles
Rev. Jean Priestley Rouas
Rev. Susan C. Smith
Yountville, CA
707-944-9361
510-483-1966
page 276

DECORATIONS AND FAVORS

Hearts Desire Chocolates
Double Tree Plaza
Rohnert Park, CA
707-585-7673
800-987-8333
page 277

Nancy's Fancy's
3480 Airway Drive
Santa Rosa, CA
707-546-2253
page 278

FLORIST

Call Our Information Line
For Referrals
707-570-0820
page 279

FORMAL WEAR FOR MEN

Presidents Formal Wear
for store area directory
1-800-TUXEDO-1
page 280

ADVERTISERS DIRECTORY

HONEYMOONS

Anguilla Tourism Board
Caribbean Island Experience
The Valley, Anguilla
British West Indies
1-800-553-4939
page 281

Anquilla Great House
Beach Resort Anquilla Blue
1-800-583-9247
page

Fetzer Vineyards Bed & Breakfast
13601 Eastside Road
Hopland, CA
707-744-1250
page 282

Fountain Beach Resort
Caribbean Island Experience
Anguilla, British West Indies
1-800-583-9247
page 283

HMS Travel
707 4th Street
Santa Rosa, CA
707-526-2922
800-367-5348
page 284

INVITATIONS

Nancy's Fancy's
3480 Airway Drive
Santa Rosa, CA
707-546-2253
page 285

MUSIC - D.J.

Goodtime D.J.
Mark Power
Mill Valley, CA
415-381-0599
page 286

Phoenix Entertainment
Live and D.J.
Armando J. Miranda
http://www.weddinglinks.com/
Calistoga, CA
707-942-9056
page 286

Stein's Grooves Mobile
Sound & Light Show
707-762-0882
page 287

ADVERTISERS DIRECTORY

MUSIC - LIVE

Blue Moon Dance Band
Ken Winett
707-795-4653
707-224-0241
page 287

Lyric Trio
Judith Anne Phillips
Ross, CA
415-459-7031
page 288

Marin String Quartet
Dennie Mehocich
San Rafael, CA
415-456-6101

OUT OF TOWN GUESTS

Madrona Manor
Historic Inn
1001 Westside Road
Healdsburg, CA
707-433-4231
page 259

Relais Du Soleil
1210 Nunns Canyon Rd.
Glen Ellen, CA
707-833-6264
page 263

PARTY RENTALS

Big 4 Rentals
Rohnert Park, CA 707-586-4411
Petaluma, CA   707-762-4444
Contra Costa, CA 510-307-4440
page 289

Napa Valley Party Rentals
365 LaFata Street
St. Helena, CA
http:www//www.weddinglinks.com/
707-963-8001
page 290

Sonoma Rentals and
Wine Country Parties
19425 Sonoma Hwy.
Sonoma, CA
http:www.winecountryparty.com
707-938-0711
and
1924 Yajome Street
Napa, CA
707-252-0711
page 291

ADVERTISERS DIRECTORY

PERSONAL GROOMING

Jacqueline Scott Make-up Artist
Amici Studio
10 Fourth Street
Santa Rosa, CA
707-579-2611
707-575-9562
page 292

Kari Ruel
Mary Kay Make-up
800-853-5274
page 293

PHOTOGRAPHERS

Many of the following have contributed pictures to this book.

Ray Baltar Photography
http://weddinglinks.com/
707-578-9300
page 294

Michael Buchanan
Sebastopol, CA
707-824-9751
page 295

Eileen Fahy
Event Photography
707-647-0420
page 296

Matthew Kenneally
Rohnert Park, CA
707-584-8077
page 294

Margretha Lane Photography
Napa, CA
707-255-2234
page 297

Leona Fern Walden
Mendocino, CA
707-937-0900
page 298a

Michael Loeb
San Anselmo, CA
http://www.piexal.com/loeb
415-924-3563
page 297

Joshua B. Rotsten
Petaluma, CA
707-762-4951
page 298

Sylvia's Photography
Santa Rosa, CA
707-542-7675
800-987-6228
page 299

Creative Focus
Georges Alta Tawzer
Napa, CA
707-255-3550
page 293

Dennis Urbiztondo
Photography
Petaluma, CA
415-766-8222
page 299

ADVERTISERS DIRECTORY

REHEARSAL DINNERS

Ca Bianca Restaurant
835 2nd Street
Santa Rosa, CA
707-542-5800
page 257

Commodore Cruises
Port of Alemeda
weddings, receptions
and rehearsal dinners
Ward and Susan Proescher
Lafayette, CA
510-256-4000
page 258

Madrona Manor
Historic Inn
1001 Westside Road
Healdsburg, CA
707-433-4231
page 259

Mark West Restaurant
2520 Mark West Springs Rd.
Santa Rosa, CA
707-528-0999
page 260

Napa Valley Country Club
3385 Hagen Road
Napa, CA
707-252-1111
page 262

Relais Du Soleil
(outside catering required)
1210 Nuns Canyon Road
Glen Ellen, CA
707-833-6264
page 263

The General's Daughter
400 West Spain Street
Sonoma, CA
707-938-4004
page 264

Mt. Shadows Golf Resort
100 Golf Course Dr.
Rohnert Park, CA
707-584-9797
page 261

SPECIAL SERVICES

Doves Aflight
P.O. Box 1701
Glen Ellen, CA
707-996-5972
page 300

Las Cerezas/Napa Wine Labels
(personalized wine labels)
Paul Carnazola
St. Helena, CA
707-963-9597
page 301

ADVERTISERS DIRECTORY

TRANSPORTATION

AAAA Pure Luxury
1221 Petaluma Blvd.
Petaluma, CA 94952
707-775-2920
707-588-8050
page 302

The Bridal Path
Horse Drawn Carriage
Ted Draper
707-546-2568
page 303

VIDEOGRAPHY

Alan Fitch Videography
Petaluma, CA
707-762-0642
page 304

Talbot Video Productions
Robert Talbot
707-765-1555
page 305

Take 2 Video
Gerry Wilson
http://www.take2video.com
707-938-2532
page 304

Video Images
Andre Cahill
Rohnert Park, CA
707-584-8781
page 306

A PERSONAL NOTE
FROM JUDITH RIVERS

Congratulations on your commitment to
one another! Trust all your plans will go
well and this book will be of great value to
you as you plan the process. This
publication was researched and written to
bring about ease and success to your
weddings, receptions, elopements or
honeymoons in the vineyards of Northern
California. Even those who determine to
enjoy the vineyards on their second or third
honeymoon, family reunion or anniversary will find many wonderful
places to plan events and places to explore in this book.

The vineyard areas are blessed with extraordinary beauty and great
versatility with what you can do while visiting. Having lived in the area
for thirty-five years and written wedding publications over the past six
years has given me insight to write this book. The phone calls into our
office from all over the world are part of the publication's answer to
questions most often asked about the romantic vineyards areas.

Wishing you the happiest of lives!
Judith Rivers

Author of five publications

Beautiful Sonoma, Napa/Solano, Marin/Mendocino & Contra Costa Weddings

If you are looking for further information. Call recommendation line on the next page.

The Recommendation Line

If you do not see a desirable location in this book, or you know of a specific vineyard setting you want access to, please read our "Recommendation Line" page referred to in the table of contents for private vineyard setting contacts. We suggest you call this line until you reach us personally. We will have the correct access person call you within a few days or inform you if the request is not possible. Pacific Time Monday-Saturday 10:am - 9:pm, 707-570-0820.

Pricing Varies Asking "How much is it?" does not always give you the best way to evaluate the "real cost".

Pricing for larger events ranges from $1,000 for four hours site use and fifty persons, to $18,000 for an exclusive bed and Breakfast for twenty overnight weekend guests then adding an additional hundred guests for the wedding. Some settings are rustic, many are elaborate and elite. It is best to ask for a packet of information.

It is very important to ask what you will receive for your money. The information packet recieved from the locations will answer a great many of these questions. It is difficult to place prices in this type of publication. The prices do change, and services are part of the package in some locations while not at others. Deposits, grounds fees, insurance, wine charges and minimums are part of the consideration. Some of the articles written do include pricing, but they are subject to change.

While some locations appear as a bargain, they may not include the tables, chairs, food, etc., while others do. If a winery, they often include a staff member to pour wine and explain the wines to your guests. Many sites provide a room to change in or the honeymoon suite. Your determination

THE RECOMMENDATION LINE

to set priorities, item by item for your special day will help in the decision making process. Be certain to read the article "Selecting Your Wedding & Reception Sites in this book".

You may access our web site at http://www.weddinglinks.com/ for updates as we receive them. But our web site will not announce a location that chooses to be private nor may not be licensed for that type of event.

VINEYARDS
NOTES OR JOURNAL

VINEYARDS
NOTES OR JOURNAL

VINEYARDS
NOTES OR JOURNAL

VINEYARDS
NOTES OR JOURNAL

VINEYARDS
NOTES OR JOURNAL